Carolyn Ambuter's *Even More* Complete Book of
Needlepoint

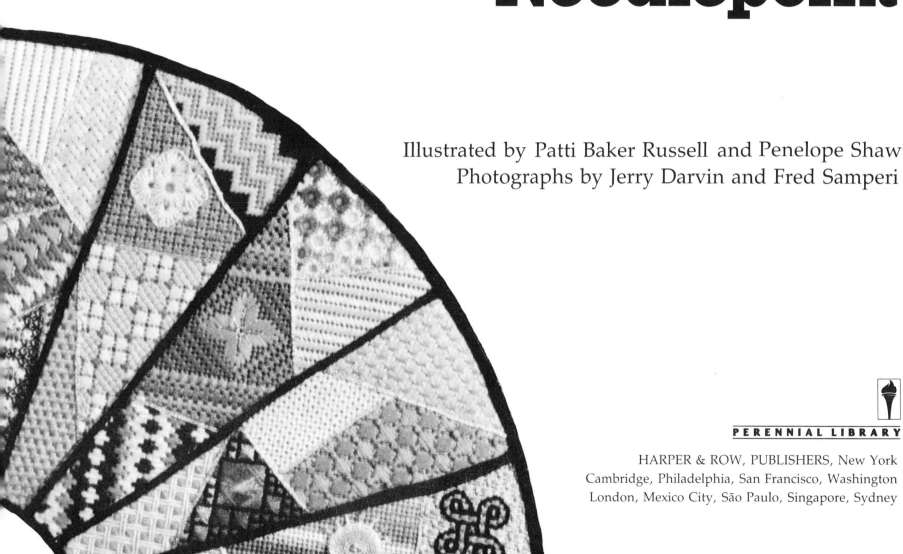

Illustrated by Patti Baker Russell and Penelope Shaw
Photographs by Jerry Darvin and Fred Samperi

PERENNIAL LIBRARY

HARPER & ROW, PUBLISHERS, New York
Cambridge, Philadelphia, San Francisco, Washington
London, Mexico City, São Paulo, Singapore, Sydney

to Sidi Hessell

This work is a revised edition of *Carolyn Ambuter's Complete Book of Needlepoint*.

CAROLYN AMBUTER'S EVEN MORE COMPLETE BOOK OF NEEDLEPOINT. Copyright © 1972, 1987 by Carolyn Ambuter. All rights reserved. Printed in the United States of America. No part of this book may be used or reproduced in any manner whatsoever without written permission except in the case of brief quotations embodied in critical articles and reviews. For information address Harper & Row, Publishers, Inc., 10 East 53rd Street, New York, N.Y. 10022. Published simultaneously in Canada by Fitzhenry & Whiteside Limited, Toronto.

First PERENNIAL LIBRARY edition published 1987

Designed by C. Linda Dingler

Library of Congress Cataloging-in-Publication Data

Ambuter, Carolyn.
   Carolyn Ambuter's even more complete book of needlepoint.

   "A revised edition of Carolyn Ambuter's complete book of needlepoint"— Verso t.p.
   Bibliography: p.
   Includes indexes.
   1. Canvas embroidery.   I. Ambuter, Carolyn. Complete book of needlepoint.   II. Title.
TT778.C3A48   1987   746.44'2   87-45017
ISBN 0-06-096064-7 (pbk.)

87 88 89 90 91 MPC 10 9 8 7 6 5 4 3 2 1

CONTENTS

A section of color illustrations follows page 160.

PREFACE

No longer a shopkeeper, but a full-time stitcher and ofttimes teacher, I have seen many changes in the needlepoint world since the *Complete Book of Needlepoint* was published in 1972. While retaining much from the first edition that is still very current, in this edition I have updated the working materials and techniques while providing new designs and adding more stitches.

Although new materials can include anything that will not self-destruct, I have described here the most practical and, when possible, the most readily available. Adventurous stitchers should experiment with everything from ordinary string to pure gold, from lace to jeweled buttons. Threads that cannot be fed through mesh openings can be couched down. Narrow ribbon and smooth metal threads can be stitched through the mesh holes. This does not mean abandoning wool. No thread is more pleasant or more practical. Beginners should learn some basic stitches with wool first; advanced stitchers should experiment with a wide variety of threads and techniques.

Since needlework is a sedentary art, I urge you to take frequent breaks to stretch your arms, legs, neck, back, and shoulders. Look at a distant point whenever you think of it to rest your eyes from constant staring. Above all else, take pleasure in your work.

ACKNOWLEDGMENTS

My sincere thanks to all the people who helped give this book a new life, especially: Penelope Shaw for her fine art work done with such good humor; Ruth Anne Gilbert for reading manuscript, offering constructive advice, and typing, all with wit and intelligence; Sidi Hessel for being my personal guru and for tailoring the Sashiko vest with tender loving care; Jerry Darvin for his excellent photography; Mary Ellen Ferree for her friendship and for stitching the Patchwork Pillow; Carol Cohen and Roz Barrow of Harper & Row for their expert care in this revision; Dede Ogden for her valuable contributions on painting a canvas and for reminding me to stress taking breaks to stretch; Kathleen Sweeney for sharing her Canvas Lace research; Gillian Moss of Cooper-Hewitt Museum for time spent showing me examples of old needlework; Joseph Ambuter and Jean Ambuter Harris for being there; suppliers who were so helpful; The Embroiderers' Guild of America, The Council of American Embroiderers, and The American Needlepoint Guild, all of them a moving force for thousands of students and teachers in the study of design, technique, and color, and suppliers of an invaluable fellowship-network among embroiderers through their publications, workshops, and seminars.

Carolyn Ambuter
1987

Getting Started

A summary of working materials plus how to do everything but the stitching—from selecting a design to putting it on canvas

Canvas

Canvas is an open even-weave fabric to be filled with stitches.
Select the very finest quality; look for strong, smooth, almost
polished-looking canvas threads. The best canvases were at one
time woven in France. The old French looms no longer exist;
now beautiful, even, knot-free canvas is imported from Germany.
Zweigart deluxe quality is the one I have chosen for the projects
in this book. The one exception is a soft tan Congress Canvas
for the vest which comes by way of Denmark.

    Listed here are the various canvases available today, along
with colors, mesh sizes, and suggestions for their use. There
are four basic weaves of needlepoint canvas: single mesh,
also called mono; double mesh, also called duo and penelope;
interlock, also called locked weave; and waste canvas. In
this book, I use the names single mesh, double mesh, and
interlock.

24-mesh

Mesh size

A mesh is the intersection of horizontal and vertical canvas
threads. Stitches are taken over or in between the mesh.
Canvases come in different mesh gauges which determine the
size of the stitch. When we speak of a 10-mesh canvas, we
mean 10 meshes or 10 stitches to the inch. The fewer meshes to
the inch, the larger the stitches and the fewer stitches needed
to cover a given area. The more meshes to the inch, the smaller
the stitches and the more stitches required to cover the canvas.

Single mesh

Single mesh is the type of canvas most frequently used today.
Most instructions for needlepoint projects, including those
in this book, are for single mesh. This canvas is constructed
with single warps (vertical threads) that are regularly woven with
alternate rows of single filling threads (horizontals), over one

18-mesh

7

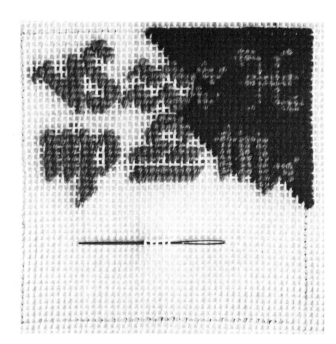

16-mesh

and under one, creating a basket weave. Canvas threads are starched to maintain a smooth, crisp surface; their girth varies with the mesh size. Single-mesh cotton canvas is available in deluxe quality, tan or white, in mesh sizes 10, 12, 13, 14, 16, and 18. Single-mesh linen canvas in cream color is available in sizes 8, 13, and 17. These canvases are suitable for all home furnishing projects, including pillows, upholstery, hangings, pictures, and rugs. White canvas is best for painting. Tan canvas is best for unpainted work, as the dark tone of the canvas sinks into the background when it is not covered. Linen canvas is the most expensive, but it is an excellent choice for work where some of the background is to be left unworked. Another type of canvas that is not so widely available but is of fine quality is Congress Canvas or Congress Cloth. This is a lightweight cotton canvas that comes in a variety of colors, in mesh sizes 16 and 24. Congress Canvas is suitable for clothing and accessories and any fine work. It is a particularly good choice if some of the canvas is to be left unworked.

14-mesh

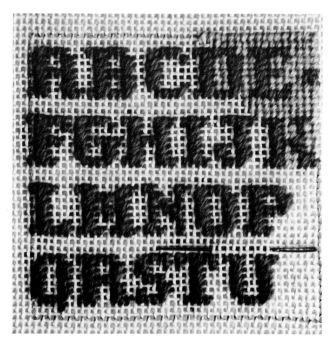

12-mesh

10-mesh

Double mesh

Double-mesh canvas has close double warps that are regularly woven in alternate rows, over one and under one, by pairs of slightly separated filling threads. The canvas threads are much finer than in a single-mesh canvas, and they are much less starched, as the denser weave keeps the work in shape. This is a difficult canvas to paint on as there is less space between the mesh due to its construction. Actually, double-mesh canvas was first woven in the mid-nineteenth century, when working from tinted graph designs and using two sizes of stitches on the same canvas was much in vogue. Cotton double-mesh canvas is available in tan and white colors, in mesh sizes 5, 6½, 7½, 10, 12, 13, 14, 16, 18, and 20. This canvas can be used for both home furnishing projects and wearing apparel. It is an excellent choice for Cross and Half Cross Stitching, and for Canvas Beadwork, providing you can find beads that nicely fit the mesh size.

The main advantage to using this canvas is that you can work the details of a complex pattern in tiny Tent (Petit Point) stitches, and the background in larger Cross (Gros Point) stitches. Petit Point is done on double-mesh canvas by pricking apart the vertical threads, thus making it possible to take four tiny Tent stitches in an area that previously accommodated one Cross Stitch.

Petit Point and Gros Point are defined here as in their original use. However, Petit Point has come to have a second meaning: Stitches worked on 16 or more mesh to the inch are often called Petit Point.

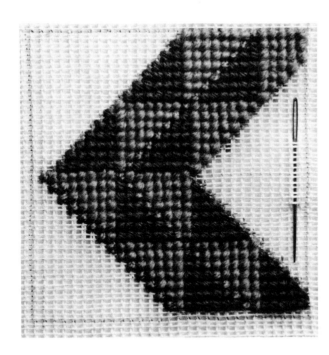

10 double mesh

Interlock

Interlock canvas has very close double warps that twine around single filling threads. Cotton interlock canvas is generally of poor quality with weak threads, and it is inadvisable therefore to use it for needlepoint upholstery. However, since it is a thin fabric that does not ravel, it is very practical for accessories. Raw edges can be neatly folded back and two edges can be easily joined by binding them together with a Gobelin Plait Stitch. Interlock canvas is available in mesh sizes 5, 10, 12, 13, 14, and 18. Silk gauze is an expensive, elegant, interlock canvas for Petit Point or miniature work. It is creamy white in color and comes in a wide range of sizes: 24, 30, 40, 48, 54, 60, 72, and 84. A fine interlock canvas called Siltek is available. It is a white polyester and comes only in 18-mesh size. This canvas is a fine choice for garment or garment trim.

Waste canvas

Waste canvas is a disposable canvas. It is constructed of pairs of vertical warps spaced slightly apart, with matching pairs of filling threads, and woven like a double-mesh canvas. Waste canvas is used in needlepoint on a non-even-weave fabric, such as denim, knit, or silk. Waste canvas is first basted onto the basic fabric, the needlepoint is worked through both fabrics, then the warp and filling threads of the waste canvas are pulled out, one at a time. This canvas is very useful for monogramming. Waste canvas is inexpensive. It comes in white cotton with blue lines to make the counting easier, in mesh sizes 6½, 8½, 10, 11, 12, 13, 14, and 16.

Threads

Needlepoint threads are selected for their suitability for canvas work. For most work they must be strong enough to take repeated pullings through mesh openings, and if used for upholstery, they must take long, hard wear. Wall hangings and pictures can employ any thread that works, but just about everything else requires threads that wear and can be cleaned one way or another. Knitting wools are unsatisfactory because they are much too springy and elastic, fine for knitting, but not for needlepoint, which requires a thread that remains in place exactly as it is laid with the needle.

Tapestry, Persian, and Crewel wools

Tapestry and Persian are the two best-known wools for needlepoint. In technical terms, they fall into two categories, worsted and woolen. Tapestry is a worsted; Persian, a woolen. Worsted is made of long, fine-quality combed fibers, spun into four loosely twisted threads or plies, that are then tightly spun into the round coiled thread called Tapestry. That is why we cannot separate the plies in most Tapestry wool. It is smooth and nonfuzzing. Woolen, or Persian, is made of shorter fibers, though they are still long, that are tightly spun into three tightly twisted plies, loosely coiled into a single strand that separates readily. Persian wool is pleasantly hairy and it has a soft, elegant sheen.

Crewel is a single strand of two-ply woolen that is tightly twisted and slightly springy. It cannot be untwisted. All of these wools can be used together on the same work. You will want to take advantage of the very different color palettes, sizes, and textures.

Nantucket Twist

Nantucket Twist is spun on the worsted system but the four plies are spun loosely enough for easy separation. Use it as it comes, encouraging its natural twist, or separate the plies and adjust the number as needed. It is very flexible because of its four plies. A single ply is excellent for fine work. Nantucket Twist has a smoother appearance than Persian when worked and it comes in a very different range of clear, bright colors— over 175 of them. Nantucket Twist is sold by the ounce and in small twisted skeins.

Paternayan Persian

Persian is the most popular wool used today. Originally it was imported, spun, dyed, and sold by Paternayan Brothers for the restoration of Persian rugs. Now the term *Persian* has become a generic word for this type of wool. There are many companies selling Persian, the best known being Paternayan Persian, which is now owned and distributed by Johnson Creative Arts. There are currently 405 shades available, which include many color families, most having 5, 6, and 7 values of a color. Paternayan Persian is sold by the ounce, in 8- and 40-yard pull skeins, and even by the strand.

Medicis

Medicis is a highly regarded, beautiful French crewel yarn that is soft and smooth. It can be used in single ply for Petit Point or it can be used in multiple strands for any size canvas. Medicis is available in over 100 softly muted shades, plus 50 new brighter shades. The only fault this wool has is that it is habit forming! Medicis crewel is sold by the ounce or in small twisted skeins.

Cotton

Cotton is the least expensive, easiest to use, most washable, and most readily available of threads. It does not wear as well as wool so should not be used for upholstery.

All but one of the following are from DMC, a very old and reliable French firm. The initials stand for Dolfus Meig Corporation. These threads have a variety of textures, with many coordinating colors. They come put up in balls, pull skeins, and regular skeins.

6-strand embroidery cotton (coton mouliné spécial)

This 6-ply floss is the most popular of all embroidery threads. Like all plied thread, it must be separated and realigned. When laid it looks very much like silk, and at a fraction of the cost. It comes in pull skeins, with 360 colors.

Pearl cotton (coton perlé)

This is a lustrous 2-ply, nondivisible, lightly twisted thread. It provides a shiny contrast to wool. The threads are soft in texture and may develop a worn spot in the eye of the needle which you should not allow to be worked. Never reuse the thread after ripping.

There are currently three sizes generally available. Size 3 is the heaviest weight, similar in girth to a single ply of Persian wool. It comes in small skeins with 180 colors, or large balls with 24 colors.

Size 5 is the medium weight. It is put up in skeins with 233 colors, or small balls with 83 colors.

Size 8 is the finest size and it comes in small balls only, with 152 colors.

Brilliant Embroidery and Cutwork Thread (coton à broder, qualité spéciale)

This is a lightly twisted, 1-ply, nondivisible mercerized thread. It has a lovely soft sheen and is easy to handle. This thread is used extensively in Slovakian and Ukrainian embroideries and can usually be purchased in Ukrainian neighborhoods. It is used for counted thread work of all kinds, as well as for open work. It is often affectionately called "à broder," as the English name is long and cumbersome. It comes in small skeins, in two sizes only, with a very limited color range. Size 12, the heavier one, comes in 25 colors. Size 16, the finer one, comes in 54 colors. For a heavier thread, use several strands at one time.

Soft embroidery cotton, or matte cotton (retors à broder)

This is a dull, unmercerized, single-ply, nondivisible thread, greatly resembling string. Like string, it has a slight twist which should be maintained by twisting the needle as needed while stitching. Because of its matte finish, it provides an excellent contrast to almost any other fiber. You can use this thread for Kogin or Sashiko on canvas, as its soft dull finish is similar to that of the Japanese Kogin thread. It comes in small pull skeins, with about 200 colors.

Cairo

This is the one cotton thread included here that is not available from DMC. It comes from a small American company, Quad-rum (formerly called Textile Studios), that is one of the few fiber production plants in this country.

Cairo is a soft, stringlike, matte finish thread that is heavier, stronger, and easier to handle than DMC's soft embroidery thread. Cairo is delightful to use for needlepoint and comes in 60-yard pull skeins, with a limited range of 30 colors.

Silk

Silk thread, an elegant luxury, has a quality that captures color like no other fiber. Silk also traps light and reflects it, so it is a good idea to use stitches that change direction. The stitches will change in value with each change in direction.

Silk thread for canvas is available in two degrees of luster. There is a soft subtle sheen typified by the French silk floss Soie d'Alger, better known by its brand name Au Ver A Soie, and the high gloss shine, typified by Kanagawa Japanese silk, which is tightly twisted and resembles a buttonhole twist.

Soie d'Alger

A 7-ply silk floss that must be separated and laid flat to capture maximum light. When this is done, stitches appear as a satin fabric. The color range is extensive, with about 400 soft shades available. It is not colorfast, and therefore if the work is to be blocked, the silk should be put in after the blocking process. This is the easiest silk to handle.

Soie Crystale

A 12-ply Italian silk floss. It is not as easy to handle as the French silk, but it comes in 20 exciting colors, most of which cannot be found in Soie d'Alger.

Kanagawa

A tightly twisted Japanese thread with a very high luster. It is one of the easiest high-shine threads to use and is colorfast. It comes in a wide range of almost 200 kimono colors.

Belding Corticelli, size A

A fine-twisted sewing silk thread suitable for couching down metal threads and as the finer of the two threads used in Canvas Lace. For Canvas Beadwork, double the thread through the needle. There are about 40 colors to choose from.

Chenille

This is a furry velvet thread that looks like the caterpillar from which it gets its name (*chenille* is French for "caterpillar"). It is mainly used couched down as it is too fragile for sewing use. I have used chenille for False Gobelin Stitch, Underside Couching, and Regular Couching, to produce an excellent velvet-textured surface. Chenille is available by mail or special order. The color range is limited. There are several weights and each supplier carries a different one.

Kanagawa silk ribbon

A narrow Japanese silk ribbon, with a soft low luster. You can sew with it or you can couch it down. It provides an unusual contrast to all other textures. Kanagawa silk ribbon comes in ⅛-inch and 1/16-inch widths. The wider is available in about 185 colors; the narrower in about 60.

Linen

Nordiska Kulört Lingarn

Linen thread has many fine qualities: It is very strong, it has a lovely soft sheen, it is easy to sew with, and it has a distinctive soft homespun appearance due to its slight uneven thickness.

Linen thread has not received the popularity for needlepoint that I think it deserves. Although it comes in four sizes for needlepoint, I list only one here since it is the only one that is readily available. Swedish 16/2 is the size; the first number before the slash tells the weight, the second number tells the plies. Linen comes in pull skeins, with 102 colors.

Metallics
Balger Blending Filaments

These are very fine 1-ply high-shine metal threads that come in two degrees of shine. They can be sewn, either alone, in plies, or with other threads. Balger Blending Filaments come on small tubes and are available in about 70 colors including gold and silver.

Lumiyarn Tinsel Thread

Similar to Balger Blending Filament, this is a fine high-shine metallic thread of good quality and easy to use. Tinsel thread comes in gold and silver, on small spools.

Balger braid

As its name suggests, this is a tightly braided thread; it can comfortably be pulled through canvas mesh. Balger braid comes in three weights; #8 is the finest, #16 medium, and #32 the heaviest. It comes on small tubes, in two degrees of shine, with about 70 colors.

Lalame braid

This braid is similar to Balger, but it is a bit smoother with a somewhat less crinkled appearance. It is available in four sizes in four-yard skeins in gold, silver, and pearl, in sizes 1¼, 1½, 1¾, and 1 (1 is the heaviest; 1¼ is the finest).

Passing thread

As its name implies, this thread passes over the surface of the canvas. It is very smooth and pliable, and quite strong. I like to couch it down for monograms or names in script. It is also great for outlining. Passing thread is available in a fine-weight size #1 in gold and in a heavier-weight size #5 in gold and silver.

Torsade cord

This is only one of many wonderful metallic cords in silver and

PLY AND NEEDLE CHART
An estimate of the number of plies to use for slanted stitches with a variety of
threads for various mesh sizes

Thread	Mesh	Plies	Needle	Thread	Mesh	Plies	Needle
Persian	18	1	24	Matte cotton	18/16	1	20
	16	2	22				
	14	2	20	Cairo	14/12	1	20
	13	2	20				
	10	3	18	Soie d'Alger	24	2/3	24
					18	4	22
Nantucket Twist	24	1	24		16	5	22
	18	2	22		14	6/7	20
	16	3	20		13/12	7	20
	14/12	4	18				
	10	6	18	Kanagawa Silk Twist	18	2	24
					16	3	22
Medicis	30	1	24		14	4	22
	24	2	22				
	18	3	22	Chenille	13/12/10	1	18
	16/14	4	20				
				Ribbon, 1/16 inch	18/16	1	20
Cotton floss	24	3	26		14/13		
	18/16	6/8	24				
	14	6/9	22	Nordiska 16/2 linen	18	1	20
	12	9/12	20		14/13	1/2	20
Pearl cotton				Balger braid			
Size 8	24/18	1	24	#8	30/18	1	22
5	18/17/16	1	24	#16	18/14	1	20
3	14/13/12	1	22	#32	14/10	1	18
				Lalame braid			
Brilliant Embroidery and Cutwork Thread,	24	1	24	1¼	24	1	24
size 16	18	1/2	22	1½	18	1	22
	16	2/3	20	1¾	14	1	20
				1	12	1	18

gold. All cords must be couched down. (Couching serves as a handsome outlining process.) Torsade is a handsome ropelike cord that is composed of a very high-luster braid twisted around a less lustrous one. It is available in sizes 3, 5, 8, 12, and 50. Size 3 is the finest; size 50 the heaviest weight, about ¼ inch in diameter.

Frames

Why frames?

As needlepoint has become more sophisticated in the use of a wider variety of stitches and embroidery techniques, so has the process of doing the work and selecting the equipment with which to do it efficiently. The use of a frame on which canvas is stretched tautly has become a necessity for the avid needle-pointer, and should be studied, if not adopted in due course, by those who have not yet used one. Certain techniques, such as laying threads with a tool, and some stitches, such as French and Bullion Knots, require the use of both hands. The purpose of the frame is to produce stitches of even tension, prevent the canvas from becoming misshapen, keep all the work visible and clean, and allow the use of both hands for stitching. Once you see finished work taken from a frame in all its perfection, you will need little persuasion to use one.

Stretchers

The easiest framing device is a stretcher frame made from two pairs of ¾-inch square wood strips. These strips are sold in pairs of interchangeable sizes that dovetail, from which any size frame can be made. Canvas is stretched and tacked or stapled to the stretcher bars. (See Getting Started.) Artist's stretchers can also be used except that these wood strips are so much wider, requiring more canvas. A stretcher frame can easily be made

at home by nailing together the desired lengths of wood strips.

Ministretchers: ½-inch square strips are available for small projects such as the stitch swatches shown in the Dictionary of Stitches.

Roller or scroll frames

This type of frame is perfect to use for larger projects such as wall hangings and rugs. They are composed of two horizontal rollers which come in various lengths, with webbed tape attached. They are fitted with side bars, which also come in various interchangeable lengths. The side bars have winged nuts to tighten the tension of the rollers. Needlepoint canvas is sewn to the tape at the top and bottom. It is laced to the side bars, and should be laced and relaced as the canvas is rolled up when a section of the needlepoint is completed. The canvas should never be wider than the tape, but it can be of any length since it can be rolled in either direction, as needed.

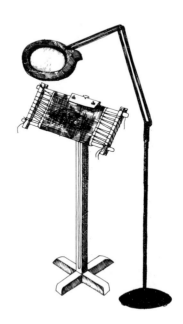

Systems to support the frame

A frame can be supported in many ways. If you work in an upholstered armchair, the frame can simply rest on the arms. If you work at a table, you can use a large C clamp. I often work at my desk with a weighted pillow to hold the frame still. There are many commercial frame stands for table or floor; there are even some that you sit on. Visit a needlework shop, or study a needlework catalog to see what is available.

Weighted pillow

A weighted pillow consists of a sack, not too heavily filled with beans, pebbles, or gunshot, somewhat like a beanbag. It can be a very beautiful object, covered with old lace or needlepoint. Weighted stuffed animals and dolls make charming weights. A weighted pillow is very convenient to use when you are working at a table because you can turn the work so readily. You can use several books or a brick to raise the frame to a convenient angle, then flop the weight so that it is half on the framed unworked area and half on the raised surface or worktable. You can make this item yourself, or restuff a bought one.

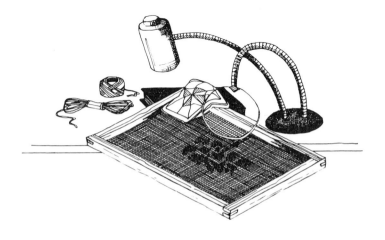

Tools

Needles

Tapestry needles are used for needlepoint. They have long eyes with blunt points that do not split yarn or canvas, nor do they prick fingers. They come in many sizes; like canvas sizes, the finer the needle, the higher the number.

The eye of the needle should be large enough to hold thread comfortably without it slipping out, and the shaft of the needle should be fine enough to draw through mesh openings without tugging. The Ply and Needle Chart suggests needle sizes for various canvases and plies.

Special needles

Chenille needles look exactly like tapestry needles except that they have sharp points. They are useful for sinking and securing couched threads. Crewel needles are shorter-eyed than chenille and can be used for the fine couching-down thread or for securing threads on the back of stitches. Sharps are all-purpose sewing needles that are used for appliqué work or beading. Beading needles are extremely long and thin like wires, too difficult to thread and too difficult for working with little seed beads on canvas. Darners are handy long needles that look like tapestry or chenille needles and are used for bullion knots or for darning on unframed work.

Emery

When needles become dull, they can be run through an emery. However, it is a good idea to keep fresh packages of your favorite sizes of needles on hand.

Needle book

A handy and decorative addition to the workbasket is a little needlebook. This is an embroidered cover with a few felt

or flannel pages inside. Keep an assortment of tapestry needles on one page, and chenille, sharps, and special duty needles on the others. Stored in this way, needles stay clean and are easy to select.

Scissors

You should own two pairs of good embroidery scissors about three inches in length and with two sharp pointed blades. Buy good ones, hide them in your workbasket, and do not use them for anything but thread. When a pair becomes dull, have it sharpened professionally. In addition, you will need a pair of new lightweight stainless steel scissors for cutting canvas.

Lighting

More than just adequate light is a necessity, not a luxury. It not only saves errors in stitching and in matching colors, but it saves the eyes as well. Rather than a little spotlight on your work, use a lamp with a large spread of light directed at your work. I am partial to architect's or studio-type lamps which have two kinds of light—incandescent and candescent—such as Luxo. They are available in art supply and lighting stores. These lamps are flexible and can be easily directed over the work. A right-handed person will find that light coming over the left shoulder creates less shadow on the work; the left-handed person will find light coming over the right shoulder is best.

Magnification

In order to achieve fine detailed needlework, most needlepointers resort to magnification. The most convenient one to own is a combination lamp and magnifying lens. One of the most maneuverable of these is called Enlarger-Lite. It has two goose-necks, one with a plastic rimless magnifying lens, the other with a low wattage reflector bulb lamp. It is a fallacy to think that magnification will strain your eyes; quite the opposite is true. Keep the lens covered when not in use to protect it and to prevent a fire. Strong sun shining on the lens can ignite a fire, burning what is beneath it.

Thimble, pliers, rubber disc

There are times when the needle needs to be dragged through the back of tight stitches to secure a thread. Perhaps there will be other "tight" situations when you need more power. A thimble helps in pushing the eye end of the needle; a small pair of clean pliers can pull the tip end. A little rubber disc is handy when you are traveling without your collection of tools.

Tweezers

A pair of small tweezers is useful for pulling out a thread or plucking out a stray fiber.

Awl

This is a favorite tool of mine. I use it to count canvas threads. I drag it across the canvas to make sure opposite sides match where they should, and I enlarge holes where many stitches converge. I also use it as a tool to help lay threads in perfect alignment.

Beeswax

Run silk through beeswax before couching down metal threads to prevent the thread from being cut by the metal. Use it on silk thread for added strength when you do beadwork. Use it at the eye end of a slippery thread to prevent constant rethreading. Use it at the tip end of metal thread to prevent unraveling.

Tapes

There are two kinds of paper tape to keep on hand. One-inch-wide masking tape is used to bind canvas edges; small pieces of it pick up fibers after ripping. Another tape to have on hand is the one used by doctors and hairdressers that is so easy to pull off. It is primarily made for sensitive skin and is available in drugstores. Use this tape to keep threads out of the way when you are not quite ready to fasten them off. If you plan to use a roller-type frame, you will also need twill tape to bind the canvas.

Hand cream

There are two exceptionally fine creams to keep your hands smooth when working with fine threads such as silk, which snags so easily on rough hands. One is called Acid Mantle; it is used by doctors to restore normal acidity to the skin. The other is a recent import from France, Au Ver A Soie Hand Creme.

Needle threader

When using a fine needle, such as a 22 or 24, you may need a needle threader. This is a little wire gadget that can be purchased wherever sewing gear is sold. They break very easily, but they are very inexpensive. There is also a thin, flat, metal threader with a small hook on one end and a larger hook on the other.

Choosing a Design

Nothing could be simpler than needlepointing a pillow for a first project. A small 10- to 12-inch square allows enough area for a simple but interesting design. It can provide enough needlepoint experience so that by the time you are finished you will have mastered many of the basic stitches and techniques.

Selecting a first design

A first canvas is a learning piece. It should have an uncomplicated design with about half the needlepoint in background stitches. Because you want to concentrate on stitching, select a design with flat areas of color and little shading. Shading is fun and gives life to a design, but you must learn your essentials first. Avoid designs that depend on outlines as these too are difficult.

Buying a painted canvas

If you feel "all thumbs" or if you want to skip all the preliminary steps and get right to stitching, you might invest in a quality hand-painted canvas. A well-painted canvas is easy to follow and you can concentrate on stitching and not on designing. The canvas comes bound, with proper margins, and you will be guided in purchasing the right amount of thread and the right size needle. Many shops help in the selection of colors and design and they may even give some guidance in stitching or offer classes.

A word of caution to the beginner buying a painted canvas: many canvases have black outlines to separate the different areas of color. These lines are not meant to be stitched and may be confusing. Look for one with solid areas of color.

Custom work

Many needlepoint shops have very capable artists who can put almost any design on canvas. Take your ideas there and have them design the canvas for you, or if you have a design in mind, have them paint it for you. It is more costly than a ready-made design, but more personal.

Beginning your own

There are many beginners who enjoy learning from printed instructions and who will have no trouble learning entirely from this book. If you are one of them, you can design your own canvas by following some of the ideas mentioned here.

Design sources

Sources for designs are easy to find. Once you become involved in canvaswork, you will look at everything around you as a source of inspiration: rugs, vases, lamp bases, fabrics, china and porcelain, and especially the wealth of printed material available—magazines, art books, horticultural and natural history books, children's books, wallpaper, prints, and so on.

Using the stitch swatches

The swatches that accompany the stitch instructions in this book are intended to be a source of inspiration and a reference guide for making stitch selections. They can also be used in patchworked fashion: Divide a large square into a checkerboard and fill the small squares with different stitch patterns. Or stitch many individual squares, as described in the Projects section for the Patchwork Samplers, and then work them into a large piece for a pillow or wall hanging. Note that Patchwork Sampler I is for beginners and Patchwork Sampler II is for the more advanced needlepointer.

Repeat patterns

Another way to use the swatches is to put them in repeat patterns. Repeat a swatch over and over again in systematic order. There are four different ways to create repeat patterns:

1. A repeat can be made directly above, beneath, and on both sides of a motif.

2. A repeat can be staggered in brick fashion in horizontal rows. Motifs in one row are side by side, but in alternate rows, the motifs are centered between those in the row above.

3. A repeat can be staggered on the side. Motifs in one vertical row are directly under one another, but in alternate vertical rows, the motifs are centered between those in the rows to the left and right. This is called a Half-drop Repeat.

4. The motif can also be reversed on all four sides when it is repeated. This is called a Mirror Repeat. You can actually place a mirror perpendicular to a design to see how it will look reversed. Look through the swatches for each stitch and you will find many motifs to use in repeat patterns.

Projects in this book

Needlepoint beginners will enjoy working on the Alphabet Samplers, where they are given an opportunity to explore a wide variety of basic stitches. If you have mastered some of these basics, you are ready to follow graphed designs such as Geometric I and II. You might also follow the graphed fan design which incorporates many of the stitches in this book. It can be worked as shown, or you can change some of the filling stitches to those you are most comfortable with. Try the Flower Pictures I and II to study the laying of silk threads and to obtain a mastery of Padded Satin Stitch and Bullion Knots and to practice Beading on canvas. Do not be afraid to tackle the Sashiko Quilted Reversible Vest; it is deceptively simple. A little knowledge of dressmaking would be helpful in laying out the basic shape, the fitting, and the assembling, but this help can be had from a dressmaker.

Purchasing and Preparing the Canvas

Selecting proper mesh

Aside from choosing canvas that is visually comfortable, the canvas mesh you choose depends on how simple or intricate your design is, or how important the curving lines are. With more mesh to the inch, you can achieve more detail and greater refinement of shapes. A simple abstract does not call for a petit point canvas. On the other hand, you would not want to work an elaborate picture or a lettered message on a large canvas mesh. A 10-, 12-, or 13-mesh is a good size for a beginner. The 10 works quickly and looks fine. However, once you work on a 12- or 13-mesh, 10 may seem coarse in comparison.

Yardage

In deciding how much canvas to purchase for a project, first determine the size you would like your finished piece to be, and then add additional space for seam allowance and margins.

Seam allowance

If the needlepoint is to be mounted by a professional, stitch a few extra rows of needlepoint all around the worked area so that seams can be sewn through the needlepoint instead of the blank canvas. Three rows are usually sufficient for soft sewn items such as pillows or eyeglass cases. For chair pads or stiffer items, such as handbags, picture frames, wastebaskets, doorstops, or desk accessories, it is a good idea to check with a mounter first. Usually the amount required is an extra quarter inch of stitching.

Seam allowance for upholstery

In planning for upholstery projects such as a chair seat, bench, or stool, measure the length, width, and depth of the object and then add to these measurements about two inches all around the work for additional rows of needlepoint. This allows the upholsterer sufficient fabric to stretch evenly over the piece, and some extra worked fabric to pull and tack in place. Consult an upholsterer before embarking on an ambitious project; you should have a paper pattern made for the needlepoint area. When purchasing or ordering a hand-painted canvas, specify both the size of the surface and the drop.

Bare margin allowance

In addition to seam allowance, leave two inches of bare canvas all around the worked area. This bare margin is for blocking the completed work. When working on a framed canvas, it is very difficult to stitch closely to the edge and you will need this margin. It will also come in handy if you feel the piece would look better one-half inch bigger, or if the mounter requires a little more fabric.

Preparing the canvas

Canvas is usually sold by the yard or half yard, and you will have to trim it to size. Here is how to do it:

1. Measure the finished size of the work.
2. Add seam allowance to the width and length.
3. Add two inches for margins all around.
4. Drag a hard lead pencil between the canvas threads to mark a cutting line.
5. Cut and bind the canvas as described in the next paragraph.
6. Mark center lines in the four margins of the bound canvas, using a fine waterproof marking pen.
7. Draw a line around the area to contain the design and a second line to indicate seam allowance, or use an awl and gently enlarge all corner holes.

Binding the canvas

Once cut, bind the canvas on all four sides to keep the raw edges from fraying. Binding with one-inch masking tape is an easy method and the one which I employ. Apply a half-inch to one side, flip the canvas over, and press the remaining half-inch on the other side. A bias tape or cloth tape may be sewn around the edges instead, or the canvas may be bound by hand or machine. If you are using a roller-type frame, bind the edges with one-inch-wide twill tape.

Direction of canvas

Like any other fabric, canvas has direction. Work the needlepoint with the selvages at the sides. Mark the top of the canvas with a T. This will remind you to hold the canvas in this position. If the selvages have been removed, it is still possible to determine which way the canvas runs. The horizontal thread is flatter and less bumpy than the vertical thread. Take a scrap of canvas and unravel a thread in each direction. The thread that is most crimped is the straight of the fabric and should point to the top of the canvas. If you have the misfortune of having to patch a canvas, this information will help in the repair.

Matching canvases

All matching pieces of needlepoint to be joined must be worked with the canvas running in the same direction. The number of stitches to the inch, from selvage to selvage, is not the same as the number of stitches along the running yard. Therefore, if two canvases are worked with the canvas running in both directions, they may have an equal number of stitches but unequal dimensions. An example: Mrs. Z. made a six-piece rug. She stitched four pieces with the canvas held in one direction and two pieces with the canvas held in the other direction. The result was that the two pieces were longer than the other four. Had she marked each piece with a T at the top, she would have avoided the error.

I have also discovered that some canvases vary from roll to roll. Rug squares or sections must come from the same roll. It is wise to purchase at one time all the canvas needed to complete a project.

Selecting Threads

Each type of thread has its own particular character. Select them for their function in your design, not just because you think them beautiful. Some threads are gently twisted and the stitches seem to melt one into the other. Other threads are tightly twisted and the stitches appear crisp and separate. Some threads catch light; others seem to shed it. As you become familiar with them, select threads for what they contribute to your work.

Quantity to purchase

The next thing to figure out is how much thread you need. The price of a painted canvas does not always include thread. When you purchase thread by the ounce or skein, it is wise to figure out how much you will need in total of each color, so that you can buy it all at one time. Dye lots can vary and when you use solid areas of color, running out of a color can pose a problem. Here is a formula for estimating the amount of Persian you would use for Tent Stitch. The same principles may be used for other threads and stitches:

1. Multiply the number of inches in length by the number of inches in width of the area to be worked. In other words, convert the needlepoint area to square inches.

2. Multiply the number of square inches by 1.5. It takes approximately one and one-half 30-inch strands of Persian to Tent Stitch diagonally or horizontally one square inch of 10-, 12-, 13-, or 14-mesh canvas. A test piece may be worked

with a measured strand of any thread for the particular canvas to be worked.

3. Once you know how many strands are required, convert the strands to ounces. There are roughly fifty 30-inch strands per ounce of Persian, so you must divide the number of strands by 50. This gives you the number of ounces for the worked piece.

4. Estimate what percent of the total number of ounces is needed for each color, then add a small extra amount to each color to make up for any error in estimating or stitching.

If you were estimating the quantity of yarn to purchase for a 14-×-14-inch needlepoint area, worked in Tent Stitch on a 10-, 12-, 13-, or 14-mesh canvas, the figures would look like this:

14 inches × 14 inches = 196 square inches.
196 square inches × 1.5 strands per inch = 294 strands (rounded off, 300 strands).
300 strands ÷ 50 strands to an ounce = 6 ounces.
You would need a minimum of 6 ounces.

Straight stitches use less yarn, although they require more plies. Five ounces is usually sufficient for a 14-×-14-inch pillow in Florentine Embroidery. Tension, the strength with which you draw thread through the mesh holes, varies from person to person, and this has an effect on the amount of thread you may use, more or less.

Color

Do not be afraid to use strong colors in needlepoint. Colors appear more subdued on canvas because of the shadows cast by the stitches themselves. When in doubt, use the stronger value. In trying to achieve the effect of a particular old piece of needlepoint, remember that it has probably faded a great deal. If you could examine the back, you would see how bright the original color was.

When you want to translate a successful color scheme to your own colors, select colors that are of equal value and that have a similar relationship on the color wheel.

Weight of thread

When in doubt as to how many plies of thread to use for a particular canvas, or for a stitch other than Tent Stitch (for Tent Stitch see the Ply and Needle Chart), make a few trial rows in the margin or on a scrap of the same canvas so that you can judge the coverage. The thread should fill the holes and cover the canvas threads without distorting the canvas. A stitch that slants across the mesh uses thinner thread or fewer plies than a straight stitch, which tends not to cover canvas threads that run vertically. Although 3-ply Persian is perfect for Tent Stitch on a 10-mesh, a 4-ply is preferable for a straight stitch, Tent Stitch being diagonal and a straight stitch being vertical. You will soon acquire this knowledge and select the proper weight instinctively.

Cutting a skein

When thread comes uncut in skeins that are not pull skeins, cut it in advance for ease in use. A good length for most work is anywhere from 18 to 30 inches, depending on the length of your arm, the texture of the thread, and the stitch involved. Open the skein which will form a ring. If it is a short ring, cut through it in one place. Persian and Nantucket Twist, when sold by the ounce, come in long rings; cut them through in two or three places. Loosely knot or twist the bundle of strands to hold them together. Other types of thread skeins are described in the Working Materials section.

Storing threads

Here is a way to keep bundles of wool tidy: Purchase some looseleaf notebook rings which come in sizes up to three inches in diameter. Slip the knot or twisted loop over the ring. A large ring can hold a whole color family. To remove a strand, just pluck one from the ring end with one hand, holding the ends with the other hand.

Storage and work baskets

Workbaskets are an attractive addition to almost any room. If the basket is of rough straw, a cotton lining will not only prevent snagging, but will add to its charm. A rectangular laundry basket set on a luggage rack is useful for large projects and is convenient by your chair. Among my storage finds is an old macaroni chest from a grocery store. The glass fronts of the drawers are handsome showcases for neatly stacked wools and antique pieces of needlepoint. Another find is a wicker baby's storage hamper on wheels. The individual trays are used to store different colors of threads and various projects. DMC thread cabinets, consisting of three plastic-lined drawers, are a boon for storing small skeins and balls.

Putting a Design on Canvas

To graph or paint?

There are two ways of transferring a design to canvas. You may work from a graph or paint it on. Graphing is very suitable for geometric designs where counting stitches is involved. It is also an excellent method for designs that are centrally balanced (where a line can be drawn through the middle of the design, and one side of it is the reverse of the other). Lettering and repeat patterns should also be planned on graph paper. If counting stitches is not for you, or inappropriate for your design, then you should paint the design on the canvas. This may liberate you from the rigid geometry of a graph and it may facilitate more natural freeform stitching.

Enlarging

If you select a design to copy from a printed source, or if you decide to follow a graph from this book, you will probably want to have either one enlarged. You can have enlargements made professionally at little cost. Take the picture or the book to a copying shop or a shop that specializes in photostats. Ask them to blow up the picture or graph to the desired size. If you are having a photostat made, ask for a positive, as they make a negative first.

Tracing

If you are following my enlarged graph, you are now ready to start stitching. If you are planning to paint or make your own original graph from an enlargement, you will first need a careful tracing of the picture. Use a fine-tipped black marking pen and trace the picture onto tracing paper. Trace as many of the interior lines as you think will help you keep the form and shape of your design, but do not get bogged down with detail. An absolute realistic rendering is not necessary. In fact, you should try to simplify the design wherever possible. You can always refer to the original if you decide that more detail is necessary later on.

Painting

Waterproof mediums only

If you decide to paint the canvas, use a waterproof medium. In many cases, blocking and cleaning of the finished canvas require a thorough dampening. If the colors are not waterproof, they may very well run and stain the threads. After all the careful work of planning and stitching the canvas, this would be a disaster.

Oil paints

Oils are a safe medium. Small tubes of basic colors may be obtained at any art supply store. You need brushes in at least three different sizes: a very fine one, a medium one, and a larger one for brushing in backgrounds. You need turpentine for thinning the paint and cleaning the brushes. Some new oils come premixed with a drying agent, otherwise you will need one. Even with this, oils take twenty-four hours to two weeks not only to dry but to lose the strong odor of turpentine which can permeate the wools. The main advantage to oil is that you can shade delicate colors, which is important for painting florals.

Acrylics

I have found acrylics to be the cleanest, safest, and easiest medium for applying color to canvas. In liquid form, acrylics are water soluble. This means that colors can easily be mixed or thinned out with water, and cleaning paint off brushes and yourself becomes a simple matter. When the paint dries, however, it is waterproof. Errors in painting can be "whited out" and corrected.

Mixing cups

Use small one-ounce plastic containers with covers in which to mix and store your colors The covers prevent the paint from drying out when not in use. Dab them with the paint color for reference. Containers can be washed and reused. If you cannot find them in an art supply store, use small plastic pill bottles.

Preparing acrylics

Acrylics come in tubes and jars. Spoon some paint into a container, add water, and stir to the consistency of hand cream. If you use too much water, the paint will penetrate the canvas to the back, causing it to buckle and shrink. Do not apply the paint too heavily, however, or it will not cover the canvas threads evenly and will take away from the flexibility of the canvas and make it difficult for the needle to glide through smoothly. A useful gadget to have on hand is a plastic ketchup-type dispenser for adding drops of water to the paint. To rinse paintbrushes, use two-quart size jars of water—one for white and light colors, and one for dark colors and black.

Tinting a canvas

I sometimes paint a canvas for Florentine Embroidery in a tint of the main color of the design. Because Florentine Embroidery is composed of straight stitches which tend to leave canvas threads showing, tinting the canvas will make them less obvious. In doing the Alphabet Samplers, which are worked from graphs, I found painting the shadow part of the letters in a dark gray prevented any canvas from showing. It was also faster to stitch without the need of counting from a graph.

Brushes for acrylics

Acrylics are unkind to brushes. Nevertheless, decent quality sable brushes are still your best investment. You will need a variety of sizes. Start with a few fine and medium sizes with pointed ends for small areas and details. For covering large areas, use short-bristled brushes with straight, square tips, one-quarter and one-half inch wide.

Magic markers and felt-tip pens

Many people have had success using these markers. Care must be used in selecting only those which are waterproof. I have never enjoyed working with them, as I find a paintbrush more accurate and more pleasant to use. Markers tend to spread their ink, making it difficult to achieve a sharp color definition. You might, however, want to use markers for a quick color stain before working certain sections of stitching where white canvas might gleam through. I do suggest the use of a light spray coat of acrylic fixative before working the canvas. Where a fine black line is needed for lettering or an outline stitch, a pointed waterproof black pen such as Pilot SC-UF may be used successfully. There is one other pen, not quite as fine, called Nepo, which I suggest be used in gray. You can test whether a marker is waterproof: Mark a piece of canvas with the pen, allow it to dry, blot it with a damp paper towel, and if any staining develops, do not use the pen.

No pencil

Pencil lead can stain threads. If you must use one to outline the perimeter, use a very hard lead and rub it off with a kneaded rubber eraser.

Drawing board and white paper

If you plan to paint your own canvases or block the completed work, a good size piece of half-inch plywood is a worthwhile investment. A piece no smaller than 18 × 20 inches with sanded edges can be used on one side for painting and the other side for blocking. Use large sheets of white paper to cover the board.

Pushpins

Pushpins about five-eighths of an inch long are used for tacking your canvas over the tracing and into the drawing board. These same tacks can be used for blocking.

Painting the canvas

Once you have gathered all your materials, you are ready to paint. Cover your drawing board with white paper. This will act as a cushion to work on and will make your tracing or drawing easier to see. Tape the tracing down next. Then tack the canvas down firmly, at the top only, so that it can be lifted if it is

necessary to have a closer look at the tracing beneath. Tilt the far end of the drawing board so that it is a few inches higher than the front edge; a pair of bricks can act as a solid prop. A good light makes it easier to see through the canvas to the design. To cut the glare, adjust the light so that it is between eye level and the canvas.

Mix the colors to be used. Try to mix distinct color differences, and keep the values much further apart than you plan for your stitching. The canvas will then be easier to paint and simpler to stitch. Select your threads before you mix the paint. Match the paint to the threads rather than the other way around, as it may prove difficult to find threads to match the paint.

Paint from the center out, particularly if there is to be a border around the design. Use as little outline as possible until you are more experienced in painting and stitching. As you paint, try to think in stitches. For Tent Stitch, paint on the canvas mesh, not in between, remembering that the stitches are made over the mesh, the point of intersection of a vertical and a horizontal canvas thread. If you have used acrylics or marking pens, the canvas needs practically no drying time. Give it a light spray of fixative and it is ready for stitching. If you have used oils, you must wait until it is completely dry.

Graphing geometric designs

Geometric designs, repeat patterns, and Florentine Embroidery are easily graphed. Graph paper is generally available in 5, 8, and 10 squares to the inch. Graph paper with 12 squares to the inch can be obtained from architect or drafting suppliers. If your graph paper matches the gauge of your canvas, you can graph your design to scale. This is not essential, however. The important fact to remember is that a square or an intersection is a mesh even if the scale of the graph is not the same size as the canvas. If you are working on a 12-inch-wide needlepoint area on a 12-mesh canvas, and the only graph paper you can obtain is 10 squares to the inch, multiply the number of canvas stitches to the inch (12) by the width of the work (12). The total, 144, is the number of stitches across the width of the design and the number of boxes or grids you must use on the graph paper.

Box or intersection = a stitch?

Graph paper can be used in two ways: The boxes can indicate a stitch or the horizontal and vertical lines can represent the canvas threads. The box system really only works for Tent Stitch and Cross Stitch. For Tent Stitch, each box represents a stitch. Colors or symbols for each color are spotted in the boxes. A basic Cross Stitch uses two vertical and two horizontal threads; this is represented by a square of four boxes.

When graphing all other stitches, as you can see on all the graphs in this book, the grids of the canvas represent the threads of the canvas. In time you will develop your own shorthand system, perhaps filling in a part of the design with stitch symbols and leaving other sections blank except for the name of the stitch to be worked.

For geometric designs (symmetrical designs that follow a stitch count), graph just a section of the design, enough to solve all the problems that might arise. (See the graphs for the Geometric Designs in the Projects section.)

Outlining a design on graph paper

1. Make a careful tracing of the design with a felt-tipped pen.

2. On the tracing, rule a heavy line around the perimeter of the design.

3. On the graph paper, rule a heavy line around the number of squares needed for the design, both in height and width.

4. Place the graph paper over the tracing paper and fasten the two sheets together with pins, staples, or clips.

5. Hold them against a windowpane in daylight and trace the design. Better yet, use a light box.

6. Separate the two pieces of paper and break down the graphed design into colors. Use a pencil so that you can refine the design until it is as close to perfection as possible.

7. Select a size of canvas mesh that will give you the desired size of finished needlepoint according to your graph.

Alphabets for Lettering

It is convenient to have a few different styles and sizes of alphabet and number series at your disposal for lettering messages and monograms on your work. Included here are four alphabet and two number series.

Plan lettering on graph paper in order to determine how many mesh you will need on the canvas. You can then paint and correct it until perfect on a spare piece of matching canvas. Or you can paint or stitch directly from the graph.

Whatever method you use to plan the lettering, experiment with various stitches such as Cross, Slanting Gobelin, and Chain.

To plan the layout of a lettered message on canvas, first choose the alphabet you prefer, one that will fit the space. Count the number of mesh each letter uses, allowing for space between the letters and additional space between the words. Now total up the number of mesh to be used in the longest line. Let us say you are going to use this bit of advice credited to Lady Mendl:

NEVER COMPLAIN
NEVER EXPLAIN

If you choose the script lettering shown in this section, two mesh between each letter and five mesh between two words, it will work out this way:

$$\frac{N}{11} + 2 + \frac{E}{8} + 2 + \frac{V}{11} + 2 + \frac{E}{8} + 2 + \frac{R}{12} + 5$$

$$\frac{C}{8} + 2 + \frac{O}{8} + 2 + \frac{M}{13} + 2 + \frac{P}{9} + 2 + \frac{L}{10} + 2 + \frac{A}{11} + 2 + \frac{I}{8} + 2 + \frac{N}{11}$$

The total is 155 mesh for the first line of lettering, not including space on either side for a border or margin. You probably would not work it on a large size mesh as the finished piece might be too large. To determine how much space the message will take, divide the total number of mesh by the number canvas mesh you are considering. If you are thinking about a 10-mesh, the number of mesh is divided by 10 (155 ÷ 10 = 15½).

The message will occupy at least 15½ inches in width. A 12-mesh would be better (155 ÷ 12 = about 13 inches). Allowing for a narrow one-inch border, you could make a 15-inch-wide pillow. The same method should be used to determine the height of the finished piece. See this message in Petit Point in a picture at the very beginning of the Working Materials section.

Artistic judgment should be exercised in determining spacing between letters. Some letters seem to have more "air" around them, such as J, L, T, and Y, and they will look better with less space between them and their neighbors. As you paint or stitch from a graph you can easily make some of these adjustments.

"Develop an infallible technique, and then place yourself at the mercy of inspiration."

— a Zen maxim

Mounting and Working the Canvas

As you progress with your needlepoint, the simple mechanics that take so much concentration at first very soon become routine. Your canvaswork then becomes a source of great enjoyment and relaxation. You are sure to find your own way of doing things, but to start, here are some preliminary instructions and hints.

Stretching on stretchers

I highly recommend that you stretch your canvas on a frame whenever possible. The simplest, easiest device is two pairs of stretcher strips of appropriate size, fitted together to make a frame. To fasten the bound canvas down, use a staple gun or tack hammer and ¼- or ⅜-inch thumbtacks. Start by fastening down on one side of the frame in the middle, then directly opposite on the other side of the frame. Pull the canvas firmly and fasten down on either side of the first tacks. Work the other two sides in the same manner. Complete fastening the canvas down, alternately tacking opposite sides. Keep the canvas taut and the warps and filling threads square. The tacks or staples should not be much more than an inch apart. When completely stretched, the canvas should be taut as a drum.

Wood side up

When you are ready to start stitching, reverse the frame and hold it wood side up and tack side down, as if it were a tray. This will allow you to work more closely to the edges of the wood stretchers on the front, and to fasten threads off comfortably on the back. It will also help to protect the front of the work.

Stretching on a roller frame

When you use a roller frame, bind the canvas with one-inch twill tape instead of masking tape because you will be sewing through the tape. Attach the canvas to the rollers before you insert the side bars. Mark the centers of the roller tapes and the centers of the top and bottom of the canvas tapes. Match and pin the center points of canvas to the roller tapes. Use button and carpet thread to sew with, and a sharp darning needle. Start at the center point each time and overcast closely to the far ends, stretching the canvas as you sew. Then attach the side bars to the rollers. If the canvas is longer than the side bars, roll the canvas up to fit the assembled frame.

You are now ready to lace the sides. Use string this time, inserting the needle into the taped sides of the canvas, passing around the side bars at about one-inch intervals. Leave long ends of string at all four corners. Tug the string on each side at opposite ends, wind it around the ends of the rollers and side bars, and make a slip knot. The canvas should be tight as a drum, with knots in all four corners. As you move to a new section of canvas, unlace it at the sides and relace it again. The needlepoint will go so smoothly and look so even that you will feel it was worth the extra work. If you use a roller frame for a small project with short side bars, you can omit the side lacing, but be sure to tighten the roller bars for maximum tension. Release this maximum tension when you are not working, to reduce the stress on the canvas.

"Scooping" and "stabbing"

When you work with a hand-held piece of needlepoint, the dominant hand sews with a scooping motion. It pokes the needle in one mesh hole and out another. Meanwhile, the passive hand holds the work and tries to control the thread. This method of working is called "scooping." When you work on a stretched needlepoint that is held down mechanically, both hands are free to stitch and control the thread. One theory is that the dominant hand is smarter, so it is held under the work where it cannot see. The hand underneath the work pokes the needle up and through a mesh hole, to be taken up by the other hand, which in turn stabs it down into the next mesh hole, to be received by the hand underneath. This is called "stabbing."

Left- and right-handed

From the description of the "stabbing" method, it will be seen that this method works equally well for left- and right-handed stitchers. One hand never gets in the way of the other, so no special instructions are needed for the left-handed person. When working with a "scooping" technique, the left-handed stitcher should turn all stitching diagrams upside down for greater ease in working.

Handling Threads

Direction

Most threads have a direction. This is most noticeable in wool, particularly Persian wool. Before threading your needle, hold a strand up to the light and note that most of the long hairs go in one direction. Stroke the thread between your fingers in the direction you think the hairs are going; it should feel smooth. Stroke it in the opposite direction and it will burn the fingers slightly. Another way to tell the needle end is to hold both ends up to the light; the needle end will be cleaner and less hairy.

Separating plies

When you use more than one ply of any thread, feed stitches into the canvas with all the plies in alignment. In order to do this, first separate any threads that are composed of loosely twisted multiple plies, such as Persian, Soie d'Alger, or silk and cotton floss. Hold what you think is the needle end of the full strand with one hand, and with the other draw out one ply. If it withdraws smoothly and the remaining plies drop downward, you have the needle end of the thread. If it does not come out smoothly, you have the wrong end. Withdraw the correct number of plies and thread your needle.

Laying threads

This is a two-handed grooming process for guiding more than one ply of thread to line up and lay flat. You will need a grooming tool, such as a tapestry rug needle, an awl, a collar stay, or a tool designed for this purpose called a "trolley needle." After securing your separated plies, bring the needle and thread to the front, at the base of the new stitch. Hold the tool in the nonworking hand, about an inch above the base of the stitch. Draw the thread over the tool and insert the needle back into the canvas at the top of the stitch. As you draw the thread, gently pull it back and forth over the tool to spread the plies nicely. Slide the tool out just as you close the stitch. As you continue to stitch, you may occasionally have to unthread the needle and separate any plies that have twisted.

Stitching

Where to begin

Unlike an artist who, approaching a bare canvas, thinks in large masses, the needlepointer must think first about the finest details. Once the background is in, it is impossible to refine or correct small areas because some of the mesh required has already gone into the background, or the stitching has crowded the few mesh to be stitched and they can barely be seen. The finest details—the veining in a leaf, the center of a flower, the features in a face—should be stitched first, followed by the design portion. If you are working on an unstretched canvas, roll up the edges to more easily reach the center area.

Diagonal Tent Stitch

Some people find backgrounds boring, and working the design and the background simultaneously is pleasanter for them. If the background is to be worked in Diagonal Tent Stitch, it is a good idea to begin stitching in the upper right-hand corner, even though it is possible to work this stitch any place on the canvas just as long as the stitches continue to be placed on the proper weave of the canvas. It is easier to keep the tension of the stitches even if one row follows the next in an orderly fashion, particularly if there are large areas of a single color. As you work Diagonal Tent Stitch, match each new stitch to the one directly beside it to maintain the same slant and the same degree of tension.

Folding a single ply

Many needlepointers use a single ply of Persian doubled through the needle. This is not a good practice. When a strand is folded in half, particularly wool, the hairs on each half face opposite directions, producing fuzzy stitches.

Threading the needle

To thread your needle, tightly wrap the tail end of thread around the sharp edge of the needle's eye, pinching the thread between thumb and index finger. Keep the yarn pinched tightly between the fingers so that the sharp fold is not lost, remove the needle, and push the eye against the fold. Draw the fold through the eye. This method may take practice, but once mastered saves time and effort.

Cotton: threading, balls, pull skeins, skeins

When threading from a ball, thread the needle with the pull end of the ball and let that be the short end of the thread. To withdraw thread from a pull skein, note the picture on one of the wrappers which demonstrates how to hold the skein with one hand and withdraw with the other. Leave the wrappers on to help identify the color and size. To open nonpull skeins, slide off the wrapper and unfold the skein into a large ring. Locate the knot that holds the ring. Cut through the entire ring just once, directly opposite the knot which holds the bundle of thread together. Fold the group of threads in half and slide the wrapper back on. The wrapper serves as a record of color and size. You can make a loose knot at one end to match the threading of each strand.

Anchoring with a waste knot

Make a simple slip knot at the tail end of your thread. A little less than an inch away from where you want to start and in the direction you will be stitching, enter a mesh hole with the knot on the front of the canvas. Emerge as planned and stitch up to the knot. Pull the tail of the knot to release it, and holding the tail tightly, cut the thread close to the canvas.

Far away knot

When you are working complex stitches, or if you are just trying something out, make a temporary waste knot, far away from the work in hand, which can then be fastened off properly later.

Fastening off

It is time to end off when the thread is about four inches long. Come to the front of the work, about an inch away in a horizontal or vertical direction. Unthread the needle, and let the end dangle in front until the thread on the back is secured by new stitches that will cover it. Or, you can bring the thread to the back and weave it under five or six stitches. Be sure to scatter startings and endings if you use this latter method or you will leave holes where one thread may be pulled to the right on one side and to the left on the other.

Anchoring and fastening off in large stitches

To start a new thread behind stitches that are too long to anchor the thread securely on the work's back, slide the needle under long stitches, heading away from the emerging point, then make a U turn and pass over the last stitch and under the rest of the stitches to emerge where desired. Fasten off the same way.

Diagonal Tent Stitch—starting and stopping

In starting or ending a strand when working the Diagonal Tent Stitch, it is best to weave the new yarn in and out of the basket weave on the back in a horizontal or vertical direction. This not only looks better on the back but helps to eliminate a diagonal ridge on the front.

Traveling from one spot to another

When you use the same color in close neighboring sections, I suggest passing under some of the stitches on the back to get from one spot to another, rather than anchoring and fastening off too frequently. You can also use pressure-sensitive tape to hold a long thread out of the way temporarily.

Stitching Tips

Compensating stitches

In working any stitch that uses more than one mesh, you will find times when there will not be enough canvas threads within the area to complete another full stitch. In such places use compensating stitches. A compensating stitch is that part of the stitch that will fit in the remaining area. Sometimes compensating stitches can be anticipated and filled in in advance; other times they can more readily be put in afterward. Sometimes it is best to compensate in advance with an extra large stitch to avoid the need for many little compensating stitches; other times it is best to work a small version of the stitch that fits perfectly.

Back stitch for exposed canvas

Back Stitch is a very useful stitch when canvas threads peep out that you wish were covered. Back Stitch between rows of stitches in a thinner thread, or a single ply of the same thread, in the same color, so that it is almost invisible. Or stitch in another color and texture as an embellishment. Back Stitch can be worked over one or two canvas threads.

Avoid split stitches

When a mesh hole is shared with other stitches, care should be taken not to split the stitch already in the opening. Split stitches are unattractive, and ripping, should it become necessary, is difficult. Push the needle into its own little corner of the mesh opening. If there is too little space, gently enlarge the hole with an awl or rug needle.

Twisting

All threads are twisted in the spinning process. Some are S twist, which means they twist like an S to the right. Others are Z twist, which means they twist to the left like a Z. As you sew with them, follow the twist of the thread. Some threads seem to untwist and need encouragement to maintain their twist; others seem to twist too much. As you stitch, turn the needle to make the thread behave. S twist threads include the soft flosses, cotton, and silk; Z twist threads include the crisp ones, Japanese Kanagawa silk, and buttonhole twist.

Shading and Blending

There are many ways of using color in needlepoint. For bold abstracts, contemporary pictures, and geometrics, use flat unmodulated areas of color. For period, traditional, and realistic renderings, where a feeling of depth or roundness is desired, use shading and blending.

Shading

The illusion of three-dimensionality is accomplished through subtle shading. Select the main colors and a few closely related values for each. Use lighter values to illuminate areas of the form that project and which in nature would catch light. Use the darker values for areas that are recessed or which would be cast in shadow. Lighter values are usually used in the center, darker values toward the edges. Study a photograph; follow the gradations, notice which areas are lighter and which darker; use different values accordingly. Notice that each value does not stop abruptly in straight lines. Stagger rows in needlepoint so that the changes are almost imperceptible. A little practice is needed for delicate shading, but if you intend to create lovely pictures, particularly florals, you will want to spend some time learning to shade the colors by blending the threads.

Blending

Blending values of thread is a useful method of shading when very close values are desired. Some threads have only three or four values of each color. Others, like Paternayan Persian, have up to seven and even eight values in a family, in which case you can shade by simply changing the values of the family as needed. I have used this blending method with many different stitches in the Alphabet Samplers. (See letters E, G, J, Q, U, and W.)

TO PRODUCE A 3-PLY THREAD

3-ply, value A
2-ply value A + 1-ply value B
1-ply value A + 2-ply value B
3-ply value B
2-ply value B + 1-ply value C
1-ply value B + 2-ply value C
3-ply value C
Etc.

TO PRODUCE A 2-PLY THREAD

2-ply value A
1-ply value A + 1-ply value B
2-ply value B
1-ply value B + 1-ply value C
2-ply value C
Etc.

Using a 2-ply thread, the blending moves along much more quickly. On a background you might want to return subtly to the first value. The effect is very much like the lovely hand-dyed wool in an Oriental rug.

The number of rows for each value must be judged according to the design. It can be done with only one lightening and darkening, or many. Or the value can be changed each time a needleful is completed. In this case, a striated effect is achieved.

When subtle blending is desired, try using some of the stitches that interlock, one row into the next, such as Brick, Back, Encroaching Gobelin, Kalem, Parisian, and Hungarian.

Blending Diagonal Tent Stitch

In blending values with Diagonal Tent Stitch, you must stagger the length of the diagonal rows. First, mark the canvas margins into the number of value changes desired, or paint in the shading. Stitch the rows in very uneven lengths, filling in the skipped rows with the next value, continuing to stagger the ends of the rows. To stitch a tiny flower petal with delicate shading, you will find it easier to use a horizontal Tent Stitch.

Shadows

A shadow cast onto the background has the effect of rendering an object in depth and making it look very real. If you do not know whether to put a shadow behind or beside an object, find an object similar in shape, place it on a flat surface, and shine a light down on it from various angles. You will then see where a shadow can be cast, at what angle, and how to be consistent in shadowing other objects in the composition.

Repairs

Most stitching errors show up quickly. Each time you pick up your work, scan it briefly. With stitches other than Tent, errors usually show up in the next row as the stitch count is upset. However, I also feel that with every completed canvaswork, an improvement in artistic quality and technique will ensue. As a matter of fact, most people, and I include myself, find when they are halfway through a work, they wish they could start all over again. Avoid this. Keep going. Every work will be better than the last. Enjoy the learning; date and initial each piece. Your work will be a record of your progress, your taste, and your skill. By the time you finish each piece, only minor corrections should be necessary.

Top and side

One of the most common mistakes made by beginners is accidentally changing the direction of stitches. Marking T at the top of the canvas should help prevent this. If you wish to change the direction, work with the T on the side.

Missed stitches

Don't worry too much about a missed stitch. I have often told beginners to omit a stitch if they are in doubt because it is an easy matter to slip it in later. If you hold the completed canvas up to the light, the missing stitches will show and you can easily add them.

Ripping

If a stitching error is made, I am in favor of ripping out the mistake if it can be done without major surgery. The satisfaction gained from regarding your own work with approval overshadows the tedium of ripping. When you have to rip a stitch or two, do not try to "unstitch." It is much more efficient to unthread the needle and lift out each stitch with the needle.

To rip out a small section of work, use a very sharp pointed embroidery scissors. Carefully slip a blade under the stitches on the front and lift the scissors up and away from the canvas as you clip each one. You can also use a sewing ripper device which has a sharp hook for lifting and cutting. Turn the canvas over to the back and fluff up the ripped threads. By removing the thread in this way, the front of the canvas will stay clean. A small piece of masking tape will pick up any loose fibers. Be sure to secure the threads that remain around the ripped area.

Patching

If you accidentally cut a canvas thread, there is no need to panic.

1. Cut a 3-inch square of the same mesh count canvas and center it behind the damaged portion. Be sure that the patching piece is held in the same direction as the damaged piece (see Direction of Canvas, Getting Started). Line up the horizontal and vertical threads.
2. Needlepoint through both pieces of canvas.
3. Clip away excess spare canvas on the back.

Finishing Touches

Blocking unframed work

If you have not worked your needlepoint on a stretcher frame, it will require blocking to straighten the canvas and to flatten the stitches for a smooth texture. This can sometimes be accomplished by a good steaming.

A good steaming for unframed work

1. Cover a wood board about one-half inch thick and slightly larger than your needlepoint with clean paper, then with several layers of old white sheeting or a white turkish towel.
2. Lay the needlepoint on it face down.
3. Pin your work to the cloth, straightening it as you pin.
4. Baste it down and remove the pins.
5. Cover the needlepoint with another white turkish towel.
6. Hold a hot steam iron several inches above it and allow plenty of steam to collect.
7. Allow the towel to dry thoroughly overnight, and remove the needlepoint.

Steaming framed work

If you have worked your needlepoint on a frame and it has a slight sag, do not remove it from the frame. Simply mist it lightly on the back and allow it to dry thoroughly. This is usually sufficient to shrink out the slight sag.

A good blocking

When a piece of needlepoint is badly distorted, it should be thoroughly dampened and nailed facedown to dry. A very badly misshapen canvas will sometimes need two or three such blockings. There should be no need for this much blocking once proper techniques are mastered.

1. Soak a large white turkish towel in cold water and wring it out well.
2. Tightly roll the needlepoint in the towel.
3. Cover a wood board slightly larger than your needlepoint and about one-half inch thick with clean paper.
4. Tack the needlepoint to the board, face down. Be sure you place the tacks about an inch away from the work so that possible rust marks do not stain your work. Start by tacking across one side, then pull it in shape and tack the other side while pulling. Do the other two sides in the same fashion. Test with a T square to make sure the needlepoint is straight. Be sure to use plenty of tacks, placing them quite closely together, otherwise you may have a scalloped edge.
5. Allow the work to dry for at least 24 hours before removing it from the board.

Washing before blocking

Needlepoint may need to be washed before mounting if it was worked in the hand and not on a frame. This process must be executed with all the care given to bathing a new baby. Use Ivory Snow or a very gentle soap called Orvis that is recommended by most textile conservators. Use the soap sparingly, a teaspoon to a large basin of tepid water. Do not squeeze or wring; agitate the water and push the needlepoint up and down. Rinse it well, until the water is clear enough to drink. Pat it dry, using plenty of towels. Dry the work flat, nailed to a well-covered board.

Dry cleaning

Mounted needlepoint can be vacuumed to keep it clean. First turn down the power of the vacuum. If the work is at all fragile, vacuum through a piece of screening. Should the needlepoint need additional cleaning, seek the very best dry cleaning establishment or consult a museum conservator.

Good housekeeping hints

Here are a few suggestions for the preservation of your work in progress:

1. When not stitching, keep your work covered with a clean cloth to protect it from dust and light.

2. Use a pillowcase as a slipcover when transporting or storing it.

3. Wash your hands frequently when you are stitching.

4. Do not pat or stroke your needlepoint, or allow admirers to do so.

5. Do not wear clothing that sheds fibers when you stitch.

Mounting

Rugs, small hangings, belts

Small rugs, small hangings, and belts are easy to mount by yourself. After steaming or blocking, press the raw edges to the back and tack them in place. Rugs should be lined with a heavy porous fabric, such as an upholsterer's linen, that will wear well and allow dirt and dust to sift through. A hanging should be lined with a lighter material, such as sheeting in an appropriate color. A belt may be lined with moiré or ribbon. Cut the fabric at least five-eighths of an inch wider than the needlepoint. Press the extra fabric to the wrong side and hand

tack it to the back of the needlepoint. On a hanging, hem the lining at the lower edge, free from the piece itself, to prevent buckling. Then sew a narrow band of matching fabric to cover the hem of the needlepoint.

Mounting by professionals

Even skilled needlepointers sometimes prefer to have their work mounted by a specialist. Pillows and upholstering can be done by a local upholsterer. When you have a very special piece, consult your needlework shop. They usually have professionals they rely on. In any event, pillows, rugs, and upholstery go to one type of shop. Hard goods such as address book covers, desk sets, and wastebaskets go to a shop where leather goods are made. Slippers generally go to very fancy shoemakers and are quite costly to make up. A fine tailor or dressmaker will make a vest or jacket, but be sure to have a consultation first to discuss the pattern and the amount of stitching to be done. Pictures should be taken to a fine frame shop where they are aware of the latest conservation techniques. If glass is used, be sure that the frame uses a spacer of at least a half inch between the work and the glass for air circulation. Also be sure that museum board and not wood is placed directly under the work. Tapes, glass, and metal should not be allowed to touch the work. When you hang your needlepoint, do not let sun or bright light hit it. The enemies of your work include dust, sun, bright light, moisture, and acid-bearing materials such as wood and paper.

Dictionary of

Stitches

A comprehensive collection of easy-to-use
stitches and techniques

Dictionary Guide

Two basic stitches

There are two basic stitches, a slanting and a straight stitch. Most people are familiar with the slanting stitch; it is known as Tent Stitch, Continental Stitch, or Petit Point. The straight stitch is known as Gobelin or Satin Stitch. These two stitches are combined, crossed, enlarged, turned, reversed, used back to front, or embellished to form most other stitches. With each new addition or variation, a new name has been added. In addition to these two basic slanting and straight stitches, there are others that are looped, knotted, or woven.

Four sections

The Dictionary of Stitches is divided into four sections: Slanting Stitches, Straight Stitches, Cross Stitches, and Tied, Looped, and Raised Stitches. Some teachers find straight stitches are easiest and so start their classes with them. This dictionary starts with Slanting Stitches because they are most commonly used. Wherever you start, note that the stitches are grouped in families of related movements; usually the easiest and simplest ones are first. There are times when the dictionary stitches appear to be in the wrong section, but they have been placed there because they pertain to the subject at hand.

Numbering system

The numbering system used on the diagram is simple. Unless specifically noted, the needle comes out through the mesh opening from the back of the work at 1, and goes in through the next mesh opening at 2 (1 is out and 2 is in). It follows that all odd numbers come up through the canvas and even numbers go down through the canvas. In addition to the diagrams, additional instructions have been supplied for those to whom stitching does not come easily. "Naturals" or "old hands" at needlepoint will find the diagrams alone sufficient. However, in the instructions you will also find some tips for better stitching and some suggestions for stitch use.

Backgrounds

Use the canvas

Needlepoint has strong roots and a glorious past, but like any other vital art, it has continued to grow and evolve. One of the important changes has been to use the canvas as an integrated part of the design. Leave the background unstitched and think of it as a handsome texture, a design element left unworked. See Patchwork Sampler II, which is composed of new stitch swatches, most having open canvas backgrounds.

Change the canvas ground

You can change a plain canvas background by painting it or quilting it. See the Kogin swatch which is worked on a white canvas painted in blue dye, with white fabric behind it. See the French Knot swatch, which is stitched through both the nubby tan canvas and the green fabric behind it. See the Sashiko swatch, which is stitched through both the tan canvas and the black backing.

Use interesting background stitches

Too much background stitching is the constant complaint of the needlepointer. However, many designs require a quiet surrounding area. One way to avoid the tedium of a large area of solid Tent Stitch is to use some of the quieter, small-scale stitches, such as Alternating Tent, Rep, Kalem, Mosaic, Continuous Mosaic, Small Chequer, Scottish, Darning, Brick, Parisian, Hungarian, Cross, Upright Cross, Long-armed Cross, and Greek Stitch.

Using the Stitches

Use stitches to simulate reality

Take full advantage of the many stitches available. In pictorial designs, use stitches to simulate the actual texture of what is being represented. Use feathery stitches or knotted stitches when the subject calls for it. A quiet, horizontal beautifully blended Brick Stitch is perfect for a calm, peaceful sky, shaded so that the darkest value appears to be further away on the horizon and the lightest area overhead, or at the top of the picture. Many of the stitches have suggestions for use noted along with the instructions. Once these stitches are part of your needlework vocabulary, you will find many uses for them. They are stimulating to use and will enhance the beauty of your work.

Stitch variations

You can add to this already large collection of stitches by working variations of them. There are countless stitches once you start to experiment. Simply rearrange them, organize different repeat patterns, combine them. You will be amazed at how original you can be in creating new stitches.

Stitch from the small graphs

Many of the stitches have graphs of the stitch swatches that accompany them. They are provided so that you can see where the stitches are placed. You will want to follow these graphs to stitch the swatches. It is very pleasant to stitch a small piece such as this which can be finished in a relatively short time. Remember that the grid of the graph paper represents the grid of the canvas. Note that all these graphed swatches have been assembled into Patchwork Sampler II. See it in the Projects section.

Stitches with exposed canvas

Another recent change in the field of needlepoint is the integration of exposed canvas within the stitches themselves. For examples of this, see Alternating Tent, Running and Double Running, Darning, Sashiko, Kogin, Canvas Lace, and Buttonhole variations. Try adapting any of your favorite sewing or embroidery techniques to canvas and you will find the even weave of canvas very helpful. Many of the stitches shown here are borrowed from other techniques such as Blackwork, Crewel, Silk and Metalwork, Quilting, Folk Embroidery, and Victorian Canvaswork.

Slanting Stitches

Tent Stitch
Diagonal Tent Stitch
Half Cross Stitch
Reversed Tent Stitch
Alternating Tent Stitch
Rep Stitch
Slanting Gobelin Stitch
Kalem Stitch
Encroaching Gobelin Stitch
Mosaic Stitch
Continuous Mosaic Stitch
Long Diagonal Stitch
Small Chequer Stitch
Cashmere Stitch
Continuous Cashmere Stitch
Flat Stitch
Cushion Stitch
Large Chequer Stitch
Scottish Stitch
Continuous Flat Stitch
Moorish Stitch
Byzantine Stitch
Jacquard Stitch
Milanese Stitch
Oriental Stitch
Gobelin Stem Stitch
Leaf Stitch
Leaf Stitch Medallion
Tip of Leaf Stitch
Diagonal Leaf Stitch
Diagonal Leaf Medallion
Ray Stitch
Diamond Ray Stitch
Square Eyelet Stitch
Diamond Eyelet Stitch
Round Eyelet Stitch
Irregular Eyelet

Tent Stitch

Also called Continental Stitch and Petit Point

Tent Stitch is the most used and most adaptable needlepoint stitch, often used to the exclusion of all others for an entire canvas. It is one of the smallest needlepoint stitches, crossing just one mesh, whereas most stitches cross at least two mesh. (A single mesh is the intersection of a vertical and horizontal canvas thread.) Half Cross Stitch, a small Cross Stitch, and a small Back Stitch are also worked over one mesh. Tent Stitch slants from lower left to upper right, crossing a single mesh.

You can work Tent Stitch horizontally (diagram 1), vertically (2), and diagonally (3). Use Horizontal Tent primarily where a single row of stitches is required. Do not use it to work large areas because it will pull the canvas badly out of shape. Work rows of Horizontal Tent from right to left, each stitch placed beside the last. Draw the needle out from underside to front at 1, go in at 2, out at 3, in at 4, and so on (4). When using Horizontal Tent in a small area of more than one row in a hand-held piece, turn the work upside down at the end of each row in order to continue stitching from right to left (5 and 6). When you work with a stretched canvas, you have the comfortable and convenient use of both hands and need not turn the work. Simply reverse the procedure and come out at the top of the stitch and go in at the bottom (7). Whichever way you hold the canvas, be sure that you are making a slanting stitch on the back of the work. Beginners may make the mistake of working one row in Tent Stitch properly from right to left and then incorrectly stitch the return row from left to right with a Half Cross Stitch. The result is very unsatisfactory, to say the least. If there are 1, 2, or 3 stitches in the row directly beneath the one you have just completed, do not bother to turn the canvas but continue on to the next row, working from right to left.

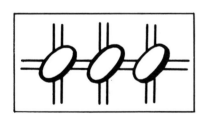

1. Horizontal Tent Stitch

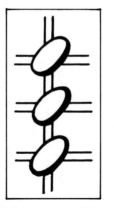

2. Vertical Tent Stitch

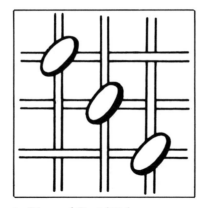

3. Diagonal Tent Stitch

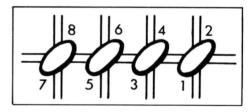

4. Work a single row of Horizontal Tent Stitch from right to left.

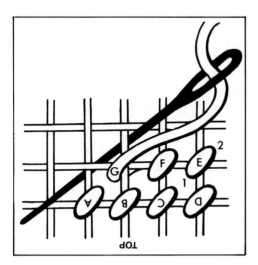

5. Canvas is in this position for row 2 with a hand-held canvas. A long slanted stitch is made on the wrong side.

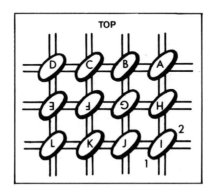

6. Canvas is in this position for row 3 with a hand-held canvas.

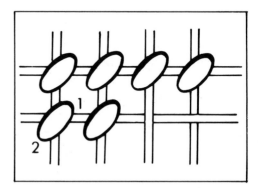

7. Row 2 for a stretched, mechanically held canvas, work a return row by coming out 1 and in 2.

47

Diagonal Tent Stitch

Vertical Tent (8) is often combined with Horizontal Tent for outlining and veining. Work from top down and from right to left (9).

Row 1.   Start vertical row with A; draw needle out 1, in 2.
Row 2.   Start horizontal row with D; work from right to left.
Row 3.   Turn canvas upside down; start vertical row with G, or take these 3 stitches by coming out at the top and going in at the bottom.
Row 4.   Start horizontal row with J; work from right to left, or continue to come out the top and go in the bottom.

The preferred and most successful way of working Tent Stitch is diagonally. It is a little more difficult for a beginner to learn than the Horizontal Tent, but it is well worth the time to master it. Worked diagonally, Tent Stitch will cause much less distortion and it can be used for backgrounds or large areas of work without turning the canvas. A basketweave pattern emerges on the back of the canvas (10). Work Diagonal Tent across the canvas in ascending and descending rows (11). It is customarily started in the right-hand corner of the canvas but you can start any place. Work descending rows over those diagonal rows of canvas threads that have a vertical thread on top (12) and ascending rows over those with a horizontal thread on top (13). If the alternation of ascending and descending rows is followed closely, you will never lose the basketry on the back of the canvas. Your stitches will mesh neatly one into the other, and you can work any place on the canvas secure in the knowledge that the basketweave will join in the end, and if you work with even tension, you will have a beautiful, unridged piece of needlepoint.

Starting from the upper right-hand corner of the work:

Rows   Draw needle out 1, in 2. Because a vertical canvas
1 & 2.   thread is on top, we know that this next row is

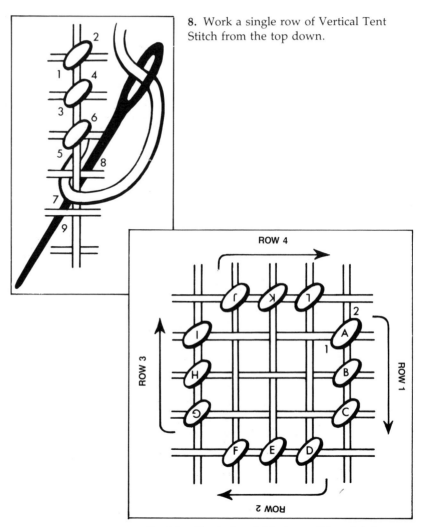

8. Work a single row of Vertical Tent Stitch from the top down.

9. Combine Vertical and Horizontal Tent Stitch.

a descending row. Draw needle out 3, in 4, out 5, in 6; end of the first descending row (14).
Row 3.   Draw needle out 7, in 8, out 9, in 10, out 11, in 12; end of first ascending row (15).
Row 4.   A descending row (16).

With your fingernail, trace along two diagonal rows of mesh. Note that one row has a vertical canvas thread on top of a horizontal one, and the next row has a horizontal canvas thread on top of a vertical one. Work diagonal rows with a vertical canvas thread on top as descending rows; work those rows with a horizontal thread on top as ascending rows.

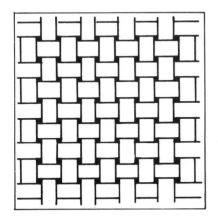

10. Back of canvas worked in Diagonal Tent Stitch creates a "basketweave."

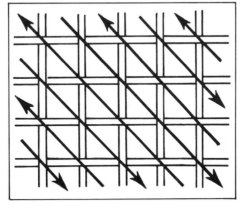

11. Arrows indicate direction of diagonal rows.

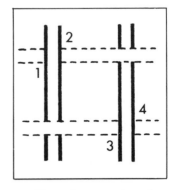

12. Vertical canvas thread on top; a descending row. Out 1, in 2.

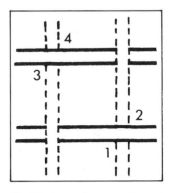

13. Horizontal canvas thread on top; an ascending row. Out 1, in 2.

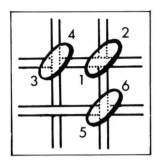

14. Starting in a corner: 3–4 and 5–6 make a descending row because the vertical canvas thread is on top.

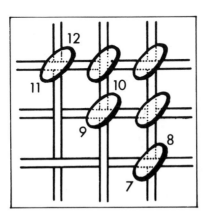

15. The next row ascends because the horizontal thread is on top.

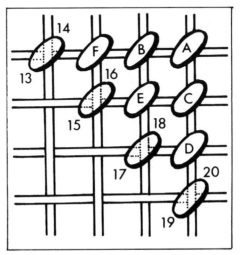

16. Another descending row is made over the vertical canvas threads.

(continued)

(Diagonal Tent Stitch, *continued*)

To start Diagonal Tent in an interior section of the canvas, you have to locate a first row of stitches. If the diagonal row on which you choose to begin has a vertical canvas thread on top, it should be worked from top to bottom (descending). If a horizontal canvas thread is on top, your first row should be worked from bottom to top (ascending). The first row can be made with as few as 2 stitches.

An ascending row (17).

1. Out 1, lower left hole of first stitch.
2. In 2, upper right hole of first stitch; needle is held in a horizontal position and goes under two vertical canvas threads.
3. Out 3, the lower left of the next stitch in the diagonal row.
4. In 4, needle is held in a horizontal position and goes under 2 canvas threads.
5. Out 5, in 6, and so on.

A descending row (18).

1. Out 1, the lower left of the first stitch.
2. In 2, the upper right hole of the first stitch; needle is now held in a vertical position and goes under 2 horizontal threads.
3. Out 3, the lower left hole of the next stitch in the diagonal row.
4. In 4, out 5, and so on.

Notice that ascending rows make horizontal stitches on the back of the canvas and descending rows make vertical stitches. If you are ever confused upon resuming work about which direction to work your diagonal row, examine the back of the canvas. If the last few stitches are horizontal, you were coming up the row; if the last few stitches are vertical, you were going down the row. The direction of the canvas threads will also give you the same information.

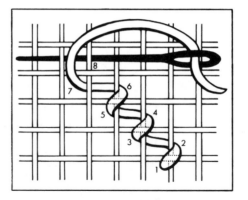

17. Holding the needle horizontally, pass under 2 vertical canvas threads. Notice ascending row is traveling on canvas threads that have a horizontal thread on top.

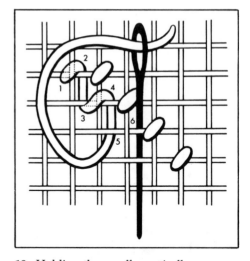

18. Holding the needle vertically, pass under 2 canvas threads. Notice descending row is traveling on canvas threads that have a vertical thread on top.

Half Cross Stitch

Also called Half Stitch

Half Cross Stitch, like Tent Stitch, is one of the basic small stitches. Work it only on double-mesh canvas as it would otherwise slide between the threads of a single mesh and give an uneven appearance. Unlike Tent Stitch in which there is as much thread on the back of the canvas as there is on the front, Half Cross leaves a minimum on the back. It is very economical of thread and produces a thin, flat piece of work which makes it particularly useful for heavy wools. Try it with two full strands of Persian on a 5 double-mesh canvas.

You can work Half Cross Stitch both vertically and horizontally, though in fact it is prettier worked vertically. Worked vertically, the stitch shapes itself more clearly, coming almost to a point at the top like a Tent Stitch. Worked horizontally, it is flatter, not as sharply defined.

Work horizontal Half Cross Stitch across the canvas from left to right. If the canvas is hand-held, you must turn it after each row to continue working left to right. If the canvas is stretched and held mechanically, simply reverse the in and out procedure, come out at the top and go in at the base of the next stitch. A straight stitch is formed on the back of the canvas, a vertical one for a horizontal row, and a horizontal one for a vertical row.

Row 1.   Draw needle out from underside to front of canvas at 1, in 2, out 3, and so on. Hold the needle in a vertical position, go in a top hole and come out directly beneath it (19).

Row 2.   If hand-held, turn the canvas so the top is at the bottom and continue stitching from left to right (20). At the end of a row, turn the canvas right side up again. No turning is necessary if on stretchers.

Work vertical Half Cross Stitch from the bottom up, at the end of each row; turn the canvas if hand-held.

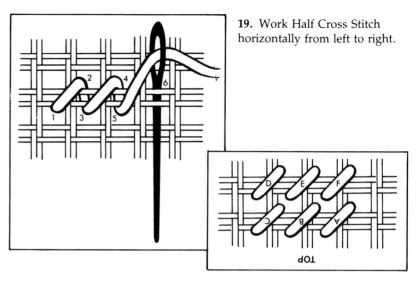

19. Work Half Cross Stitch horizontally from left to right.

20. Canvas is in this position for row 2.

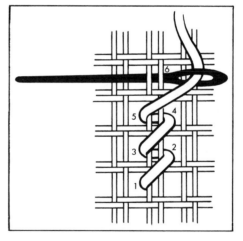

21. Work Half Cross Stitch vertically from bottom to top.

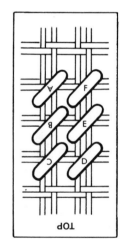

22. Canvas is in this position for row 2.

Row 1.   Draw needle out 1, in 2, out 3. Hold needle in a horizontal position; go in to the right of the double threads and come out directly beside them (21).

Row 2.   Turn the canvas and continue stitching from the bottom up (22).

51

Reversed Tent Stitch

Reversed Tent Stitch is a pattern stitch that resembles knitting. It is composed of two rows of Tent Stitch and each row slants in an opposite direction.

Work it horizontally (23) or vertically (24). Reversed Tent Stitch is a useful background stitch worked entirely in one color, in shaded rows of a single color, or blended rows of many colors and values. Use two contrasting colors to create a herringbone stripe, as seen in the accompanying swatch where the herringbone stripes are worked into a woven ribbon design. Because the two rows of stitches slant in opposite directions, the canvas between the rows can be unpleasantly exposed, making it necessary therefore to select a heavyweight thread. (See Reversed Tent Stitch in section A2 of the Fan Sampler.)

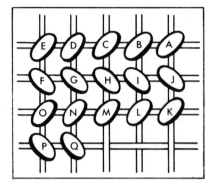

23. Work Reversed Tent Stitch in horizontal rows.

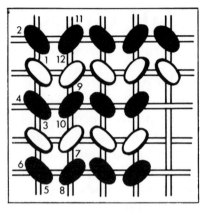

24. Work Reversed Tent Stitch in vertical rows. Create a horizontal herringbone stripe by stitching every other mesh and later filling the empty mesh with a second color.

Reversed Tent Stitch creates herringbone stripes in woven ribbon pattern using 3-ply Persian. On 24-mesh.

Alternating Tent Stitch

Alternating Tent Stitch is a pattern stitch composed of Tent Stitch that alternately slants in one direction, then the other, as you work it in horizontal rows which also alternate (25).

Canvas is exposed but it becomes an integral part of the stitch pattern. Try Alternating Tent Stitch over two canvas threads, both horizontally and vertically, thus enlarging the stitch and exposing more canvas. (See Alternating Tent Stitch in section B2 of the Fan Sampler.)

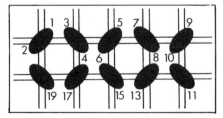

25. Work Alternating Tent Stitch in horizontal rows. Note that the stitches alternate direction vertically as well as horizontally.

Rep Stitch

Also called Aubusson Stitch

Rep Stitch is an unusual background stitch that looks like a Rep fabric or an Aubusson tapestry. It is a very appropriate stitch to use for an entire wall hanging in either period or modern style.

    You can work Rep Stitch diagonally (26) or vertically (27), on either single- or double-mesh canvas. When working on a double mesh, do not split the double vertical canvas threads, but do stitch over the individual horizontal ones. By doing this you achieve a very fine-textured stitch without the tedium of splitting vertical threads. If you are not working on a stretched canvas, you must turn your canvas after each vertical row. You can avoid turning the canvas if you work the Rep Stitch diagonally.

Rep Stitch boxes using 2-ply Persian. On 10 double mesh.

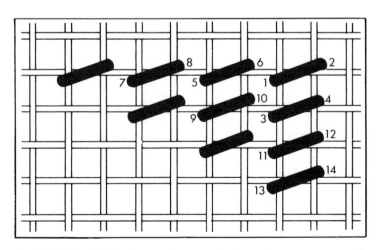

26. Work Rep Stitch diagonally on a single mesh.

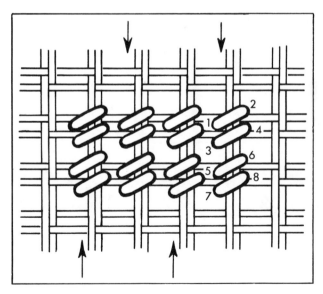

27. Work Rep Stitch vertically on a double mesh.

Slanting Gobelin Stitch

Also called Sloping Gobelin and Oblique Gobelin Stitch

Slanting Gobelin is actually a large Tent Stitch worked over 2, 3, 4, or 5 horizontal canvas threads and over 1, 2, or 3 vertical canvas threads, in any combination. Work one row from right to left, and the next from left to right, following the numbers in the diagrams. The work may also be turned upside down if this is easier, and all the rows worked in the same direction. Remember to be consistent in your stitching. Work over the same number of horizontal and vertical canvas threads within each row.

   Note in diagrams 28, 29, and 32 that Tent Stitch is taken at the beginning and end of each row. They are compensating stitches used to cover the canvas threads that would otherwise be exposed.

   You can work Slanting Gobelin Stitch equally well in vertical rows. Use it for geometric designs, borders, and for quickly worked backgrounds. For a lush grassy background for animals on pictures and pillows, try two values of green wool and slant the stitch over one vertical canvas thread, as in diagrams 30 and 31. This stitch is used as a part of many of the composite stitches that follow.

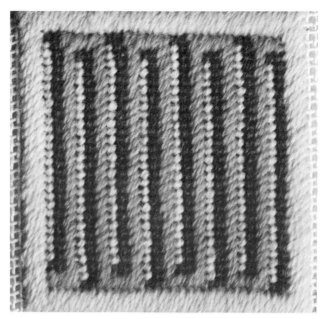

Slanting Gobelin Stitch in long vertical rows connect in "U" turns in 3-ply Persian. Tent Stitch fills spaces using 2-ply Persian. On 12-mesh.

   Note long diagonal stitches avoid breaks in upper left and lower right corners.

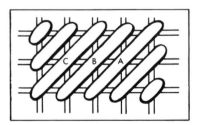

30. Slanting Gobelin Stitch over 2 horizontal by 1 vertical canvas thread.

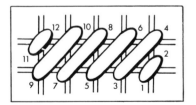

28. Work Slanting Gobelin Stitch over 2 horizontal by 2 vertical canvas threads.

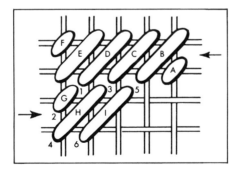

29. Work row 1 from right to left; row 2 from left to right.

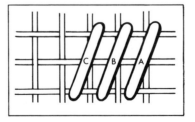

31. Slanting Gobelin Stitch over 3 horizontal by 1 vertical canvas thread.

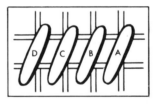

32. Slanting Gobelin Stitch over 3 horizontal by 3 vertical canvas threads. Note compensating Tent Stitch at either end of the row.

Kalem Stitch

Also called Knitting Stitch

Kalem Stitch resembles knitting. There are two other stitches that also look like knitting: Reversed Tent Stitch and Chain Stitch.

For a vertical knit effect, work from the top of the canvas down for one row and from the bottom up for the next row; it is not necessary to turn the canvas. Take stitches over 1 vertical by 2 horizontal canvas threads (33).

For a horizontal effect, work from side to side, following the numbers in the diagram. Take stitches over 2 vertical by 1 horizontal canvas thread (34). Use finer thread than for most stitches on the same size mesh as this stitch has excellent coverage. (See Kalem Stitch in section I2 of the Fan Sampler.)

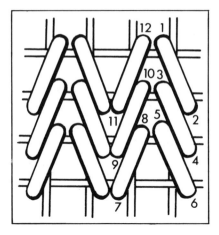

33. Kalem Stitch in vertical rows.

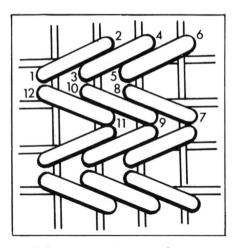

34. Kalem Stitch in horizontal rows.

Kalem Stitch in horizontally and vertically worked ribbons with a Tent Stitch ground, using 2-ply Persian. On 12-mesh.

Encroaching Gobelin Stitch

Encroaching Gobelin is a variation of Slanting Gobelin. The second row of stitches overlaps or encroaches into the row above. The encroaching must be done with care. Consistently insert the needle one canvas thread up and to the right between the stitches in the row above (35). If you are using wool, take care not to split the stitches as you enter the row above. Note in diagram 36 that the two rows of stitches are worked in alternate directions, rather than turning the canvas in order to enter the row above at the top of the stitch.

Use Encroaching Gobelin in small areas, particularly on an unstretched canvas, since this stitch tends to distort canvas. The overlapping makes it an excellent choice for the subtle shading of fur and feathers.

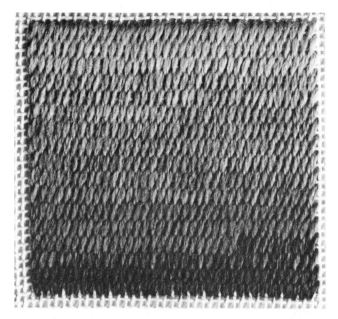

Encroaching Gobelin Stitch with rows subtly blended, using 2-ply Persian. On 12-mesh.

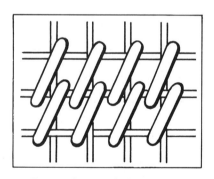

35. Encroaching Gobelin Stitch over 1 vertical by 2 horizontal canvas threads.

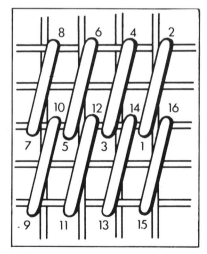

36. Encroaching Gobelin Stitch over 1 vertical by 3 horizontal canvas threads.

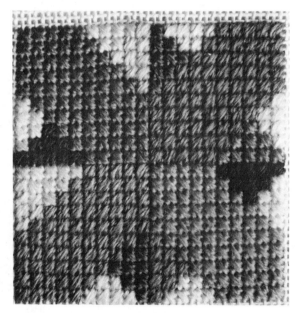

Mosaic Stitch slants toward center in each quarter, using 2-ply Persian. On 14-mesh.

Mosaic Stitch

Also called Diagonal Hungarian Stitch

Mosaic Stitch is a unit of three stitches: Tent, Slanting Gobelin, and another Tent (37).

It can be worked in horizontal rows from right to left (38), in vertical rows from the top down (you may turn the work with each row) (39), and in diagonal rows (40). Working this stitch in diagonal rows creates the least distortion.

Mosaic Stitch is an excellent background stitch, particularly around Tent Stitch where the compensating Tent Stitches fit into the design. Experiment with alternate rows of a different color or value for a checkerboard pattern. For a lace effect, you can stitch only alternate diagonal rows, leaving squares of open canvas (41). Or, after leaving alternate rows open, you can give the canvas a quarter turn and fill the open squares with Mosaic Stitches slanting in the opposite direction (42). (See Mosaic Stitch in a border of Flower Pictures I and II.)

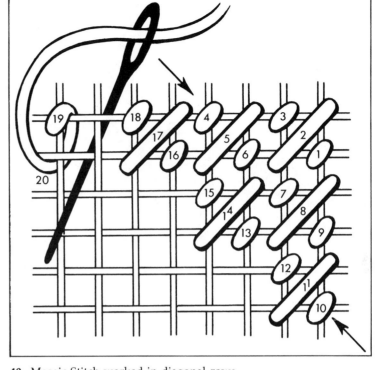

40. Mosaic Stitch worked in diagonal rows.

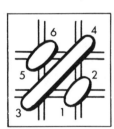

37. Mosaic Stitch worked from the lower right corner.

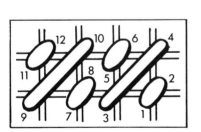

38. Mosaic Stitch worked in a horizontal row.

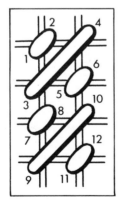

39. Mosaic Stitch worked in a vertical row.

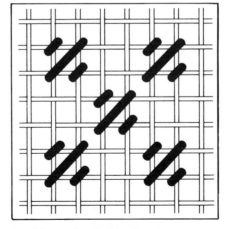

41. Mosaic Stitch skipping alternate diagonal rows.

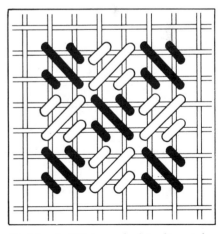

42. Mosaic Stitch worked in diagonal rows, traveling in opposite directions.

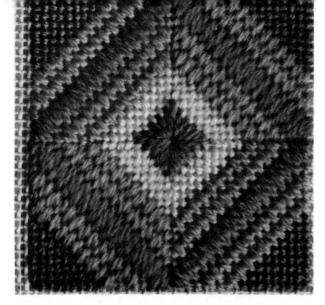

Continuous Mosaic Stitch slants in two directions in diamond shape, with Diamond Eyelet center. Tent Stitch ground matches slant of Continuous Mosaic Stitch, using 2-ply Persian. On 12-mesh.

Continuous Mosaic Stitch

Also called Diagonal Mosaic Stitch and Diagonal Florentine Stitch

Continuous Mosaic Stitch is like a Mosaic Stitch worked in diagonal rows, except that there is only one short stitch between the units. It is a handsome background stitch, although it distorts the canvas unless the canvas is stretched on a frame. A good blocking will straighten the canvas, however.

Alternate short and long stitches in diagonal rows (43). Vary the Continuous Mosaic Stitch by alternating the lengths of the Slanting Gobelin Stitch (44) and (45). Maintain a straight edge with the help of this formula for the counted placement of the compensating Tent Stitch: Work 1 long (Gobelin Stitch) and 2 short (Tent Stitch) along the edges (46). (See Continuous Mosaic in Geometrics I and II.)

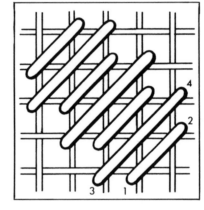

43. Continuous Mosaic with a stitch count over 1, then 2.

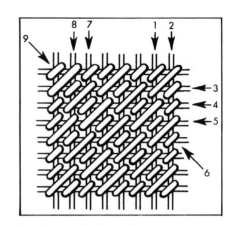

46. A formula for adding compensating stitches to make a straight edge, starting at the top of the first Mosaic Stitch:

1. Tent
2. Slanting Gobelin
3. Tent. This completes the corner Mosaic Stitch.
4. Compensating Tent
5. Skip this canvas thread.
6. Tent, Slanting Gobelin; alternate the two stitches, traveling upward to end of diagonal row.
7. Compensating Tent
8. Skip this canvas thread.
9. Tent, Slanting Gobelin; alternate the two stitches, traveling downward to the end of the second diagonal row.

44. Continuous Mosaic Stitch with a stitch count over 2, then 3.

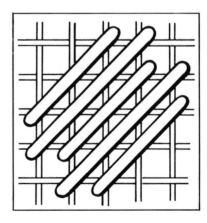

45. Continuous Mosaic Stitch with a stitch count over 3, then 4.

Long Diagonal Stitch

Long Diagonal Stitch is similar to Continuous Mosaic except that the Slanting Gobelin is made over the same number of mesh.

Work this stitch in alternating diagonal rows with pairs of Slanting Gobelin Stitch, one above and one beside the other (47). To maintain a straight edge, work 2 compensating Tent Stitch and 2 Slanting Gobelin Stitch at each edge (48). (See Long Diagonal Stitch in Geometric Designs I and II.)

Small Chequer Stitch, using 3-ply Persian. On 10-mesh.

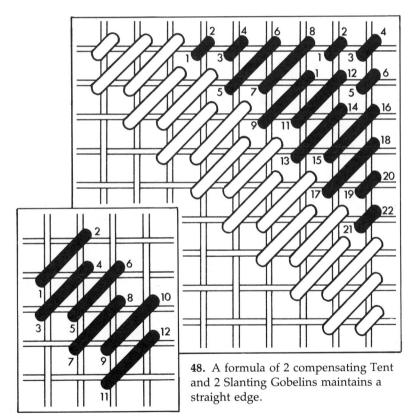

48. A formula of 2 compensating Tent and 2 Slanting Gobelins maintains a straight edge.

47. Pairs of Slanting Gobelins travel in diagonal rows.

Small Chequer Stitch

Small Chequer Stitch is a combination of Mosaic Stitch units and boxes of 4 Tent Stitch.

Work Mosaic Stitch in diagonal rows, skip a set of 2 by 2 canvas threads between each row and fill them later with Tent Stitch (49). This is a good background stitch and is most striking when worked in two colors or two values. (See Small Chequer in section I1 of the Fan Sampler.)

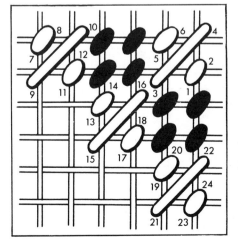

49. Alternate diagonal rows of Mosaic with boxes of Diagonal Tent.

59

Cashmere Stitch

Cashmere Stitch is Mosaic Stitch made with the addition of a second Slanting Gobelin. Units are composed of 4 stitches instead of 3 (50).

Work Cashmere Stitch in horizontal or vertical rows; if you work in diagonal rows there is less distortion of the canvas (51). This is a good background stitch that resembles a woven fabric. Boxes can be worked in different colors or values as in letter X of the Alphabet Sampler.

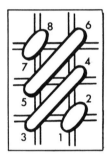

50. Units of Cashmere Stitch worked horizontally start at the base of a unit; units worked vertically start at the top. Turn work with each row or reverse order in which stitches are taken.

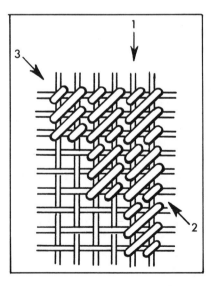

51. Start a vertical row or a corner of a diagonal row at 1. First stitch of first (ascending) diagonal row starts at 2. First stitch of second (descending) diagonal row starts at 3.

Continuous Cashmere Stitch

Continuous Cashmere Stitch is similar to a Cashmere Stitch worked in diagonal rows except that there is only one short stitch between the units. Drop each new diagonal row one canvas thread as you repeat the last diagonal row (52). Work compensating stitches afterward to make straight edges.

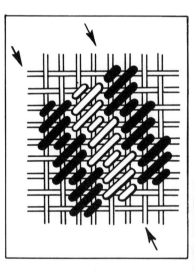

52. Diagonal rows of Continuous Cashmere are worked alternately from top to bottom and bottom to top. Note that in every other row units of Cashmere Stitch are parallel.

Cashmere Stitch border. frames center area of Continuous Cashmere using 2-ply Persian. On 12-mesh.

Flat Stitch

Also called Diagonal Satin Stitch and Scotch Stitch

Flat Stitch is a square unit of 5 or 7 slanting stitches, worked over 3 by 3 or 4 by 4 canvas threads (53). Work Flat Stitch in horizontal or vertical rows. It does distort the canvas, so when covering large areas it is better to work in diagonal rows.

For a checkered effect, with alternate boxes slanting in opposite directions, work in just one direction first, skipping every other set of diagonal rows (54). When ready to work in the other direction, give the canvas a quarter turn so that the top is at the side. Your stitches will now travel in the opposite direction (55). Flat Stitch combines nicely with other stitches such as Cashmere Stitch (56). Try Flat Stitch in various values of the same color, or add Back Stitch or Cross Stitch between the units. (See Flat with Cashmere in section H2 of the Fan Sampler.)

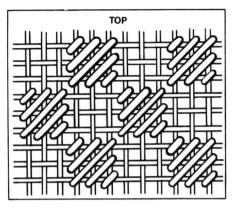

54. Complete the stitches traveling in one direction first when working alternate rows that travel in both directions.

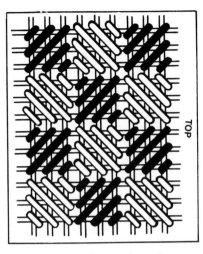

55. Then turn the work so that the top is at the side and fill the remaining rows.

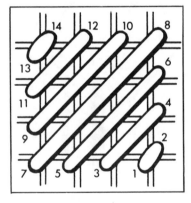

53. Flat Stitch over 4 horizontal by 4 vertical canvas threads with 7 stitches to the unit.

Flat Stitch distortion creates striking effect in woven ribbon pattern. Ribbon of 7 Flat Stitches, edged on each side with two rows Tent and one row Slanting Gobelin. Canvas given quarter turn to change direction, using 3-ply Persian. On 10-mesh.

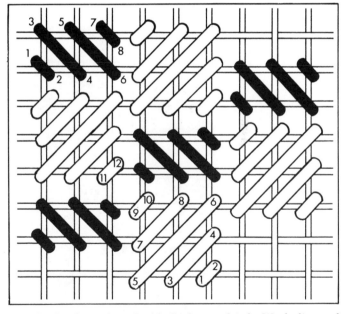

56. Flat Stitch combined with Cashmere Stitch. Work diagonal rows of Flat Stitch so that each row is 3 canvas threads from the last row on either side but is only 2 threads away vertically. Fill the spaces with Cashmere Stitch.

61

Cushion Stitch

Cushion Stitch is a unit of 4 Flat Stitch. It is a very useful stitch for background or border, and is very easy to master. Work 2 Flat Stitch in a diagonal row, then a long stitch between them (57). Give the canvas a quarter turn so that the top becomes the side and work a second set of Flat Stitch over the laid stitch (58). You can alternate boxes of Cushion Stitch with boxes of Tent Stitch or any stitch that occupies the same number of canvas threads. (See Cushion Stitch in section B3 of the Fan Sampler.)

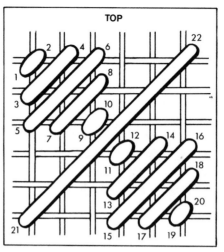

57. Work 2 Flat Stitches, then a long stitch between them.

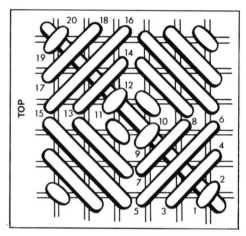

58. With the top at the side, work 2 Flat Stitches over the long stitch.

Cushion Stitch boxes using 2-ply Persian. On 12-mesh.

Large Chequer Stitch in two sizes using 3-ply Persian for Flat Stitch and 2-ply for Tent Stitch. Interior checks over 3 by 3 canvas threads, remainder over 4 by 4. On 12-mesh.

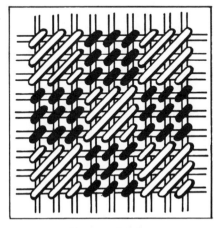

59. Large Chequer Stitch over 3 horizontal by 3 vertical canvas threads.

Large Chequer Stitch

Large Chequer Stitch is composed of Flat Stitch alternating with boxes of Tent Stitch.

Work diagonal rows of Flat Stitch, skipping an equal set of canvas threads; fill them in later with Tent Stitch. This is a very easy stitch and it is particularly attractive when done in two colors (59 and 60).

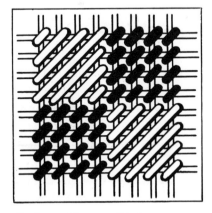

60. Large Chequer Stitch over 4 horizontal by 4 vertical canvas threads.

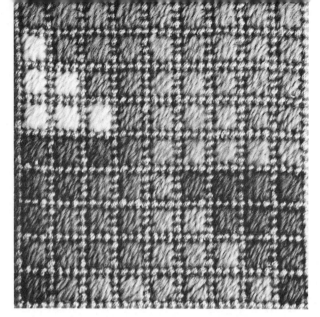

Scottish Stitch checkerboard using 2-ply Persian for Flat Stitch and 7-ply French silk for Tent Stitch. On 12-mesh.

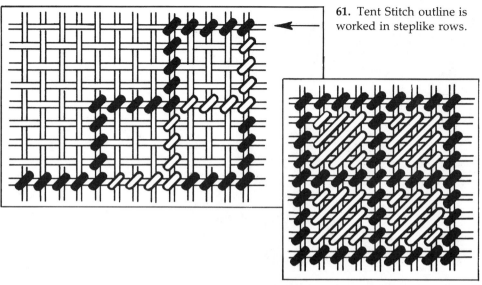

61. Tent Stitch outline is worked in steplike rows.

62. Flat Stitch fills the open squares.

Scottish Stitch

Scottish Stitch is a Flat Stitch outlined with Tent Stitch.

To avoid distortion, work the Tent Stitch first in steplike rows (61), then fill the squares with Flat Stitch in diagonal rows (62). If you reverse the direction of the Flat Stitch in every other row, you will eliminate the distortion. To accomplish this, give the canvas a quarter turn so that the top is on the side.

If you plan to work the outline and Flat Stitch in the same thread, enter the Flat Stitch first, put in a corner Tent Stitch before and after each Flat unit, as in diagram (63). Flat Stitch can also be taken over 4 canvas threads, but you will have to take 6 Tent Stitch in each step to enlarge the square openings.

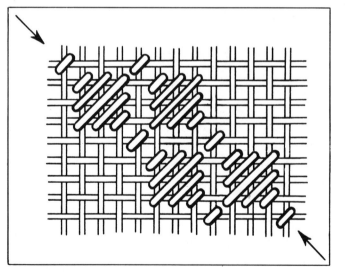

63. When working Scottish Stitch in one thread, work the Flat Stitch and corner Tent Stitch in the same diagonal row. Later fill vertical and horizontal rows with Tent Stitch.

Continuous Flat Stitch in bold stripes with Mosaic Stitch in two corners, using 2-ply Persian. On 12-mesh.

Moorish Stitch

Moorish Stitch is a variation of Continuous Flat Stitch. Work a diagonal row of Continuous Flat Stitch (2, 3, 4, 3), then outline it on either side with steps of Tent Stitch (65). Try this attractive background stitch using contrasting textures and colors for the Flat and the Tent. (See letters E and Y of the Alphabet Sampler.)

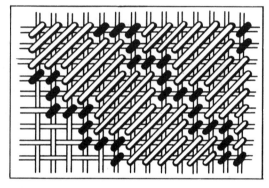

65. Note compensating stitches are used to keep both edges straight. Tent Stitch steps are composed of 3 stitches in each step; count the end stitch for each step.

Continuous Flat Stitch
Also called Diagonal Flat Stitch and Diagonal Stitch

Continuous Flat Stitch travels across the canvas in diagonal rows, over 2, 3, 4, 3 canvas threads for each repeat. Note in diagram (64) that the longest stitches in one row are diagonally opposite the shortest stitches in the next row.

Use Continuous Flat Stitch to produce a rich brocade fabric. It is especially handsome worked in bold stripes of color. Like all long diagonal stitches, it distorts the canvas unless it is well stretched on a frame. (See Continuous Flat in section F1 of the Fan Sampler.)

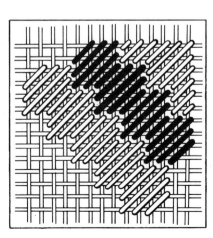

64. Note that compensating stitches are added at top and side edge of the first row.

Moorish Stitch, using 2-ply Persian with size 3 pearl cotton accent. On 12-mesh.

65

Byzantine Stitch

Byzantine Stitch is the simplest of the zigzag stitches.
It is easy to start if you work a Flat Stitch over a square of 4
canvas threads in the corner (66). Work diagonal rows of stitches
in steps across the canvas: Count over 8 canvas threads to the
left of the corner Flat Stitch and work an elongated Flat Stitch
until you come to the upper corner of the original Flat Stitch,
then work a vertical row until you come to the lower corner
of the Flat Stitch. Work a consistent pattern of 5 horizontal and
5 vertical Slanting Gobelin Stitch as a formula.

For a less rigid design, you can start anyplace on the
canvas; establish a single row of any count or size, then follow
its course with subsequent rows. (See Byzantine in section H5 of
the Fan Sampler.)

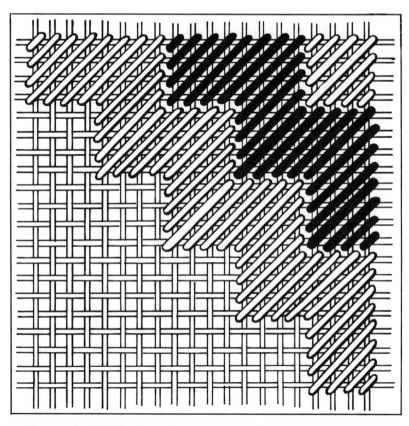

66. Start with a Flat Stitch in the corner over 4 by 4 canvas threads.

Byzantine Stitch over 4 canvas threads, with a formula of 5 Slanting Gobelins for each step, using
2-ply Persian. Note Flat Stitch in corner. On 12-mesh.

Jacquard Stitch

Jacquard Stitch is composed of Slanting Gobelin steps outlined with Tent Stitch.

Work Slanting Gobelin over 2 by 2 canvas threads in steps of a constant, predetermined number of stitches. Diagram 67 has a count of 5 stitches to a step. Steps of 4, 6, or 7 stitches are also possible. For a more freely worked piece, you might exaggerate the steps and make them in many different lengths. Use compensating stitches to keep edges straight or to fill in any open canvas.

When you are in position to work a horizontal row of Tent Stitch and the row travels from left to right, come out at the top of the stitch and go in at the base. (See Jacquard Stitch in section D1 of the Fan Sampler.)

Jacquard Stitch with 5 Slanting Gobelins, using 2-ply Persian; 5 Tent Stitches, using 7-ply French silk for each step. On 12-mesh.

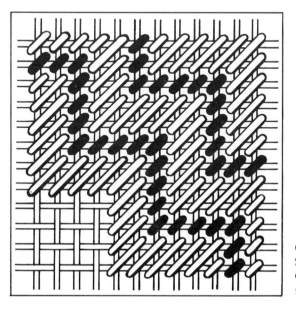

67. Each plane is composed of 5 Slanting Gobelins and 5 Tent Stitches. Compensating stitches square off the edges.

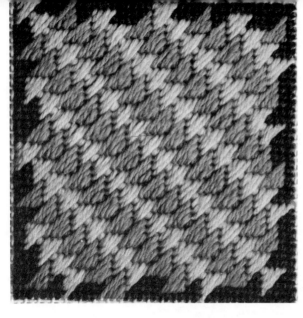

Milanese Stitch using matte cotton in 2 colors. There are no compensating stitches. Tent Stitch fills extra canvas in contrasting color. On 14-mesh.

Milanese Stitch

Milanese Stitch may be thought of as half a Flat Stitch. Work each unit with 4 stitches.

The units look like arrowheads; work them in diagonal rows across the canvas, each row pointing in the opposite direction from the last. Note in diagram 68 that the shortest stitch in one row is diagonally opposite the longest stitch in the next row. Use compensating stitches to fill the open mesh in the upper right corner. Work Milanese Stitch in one or two colors. (See it in letter Z of the Alphabet Sampler.)

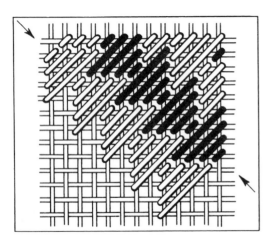

68. Work half of a Flat Stitch with the Tent Stitch on top for one row, and half of a Flat with a Tent at the base for the next.

Oriental Stitch

Oriental Stitch is a Milanese Stitch with Slanting Gobelin wedged between each diagonal row.

Note that you take the longest stitch in one row diagonally opposite the longest stitch in the next row (69). Arrowheads point in opposite directions as in Milanese. Work the rows of Milanese first, then fill the open canvas with Slanting Gobelin, perhaps in a contrasting color. (Oriental Stitch may be seen in letter W of the Alphabet Sampler.)

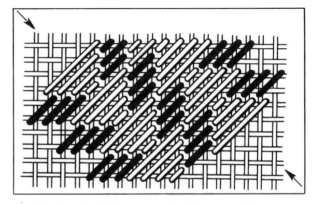

69. Slanting Gobelins are worked horizontally in one diagonal row and vertically in the next.

Oriental Stitch using 2-ply Persian. No compensating stitches; additional Slanting Gobelins fill extra canvas. On 12-mesh.

Gobelin Stem Stitch

Also called Stem Stitch

Gobelin Stem Stitch combines vertical rows of Gobelin slanting in opposite directions, with Back Stitch taken between each vertical row.

Stitch Slanting Gobelin over 2 horizontal by 2 vertical canvas threads. Work in vertical rows, alternating directions (70). Note that there are different numbering systems for the pairs of up and down rows. The first pair of rows, one traveling up and one down, produces longer stitches on the back, resulting in a heavier backing and using more thread. The pair on the right produces shorter stitches on the back, resulting in a thinner fabric.

Work the Gobelin first, then work the Back Stitch over 1 or 2 canvas threads. You can emphasize the Back Stitch with the use of contrasting thread. (See the letter T in the Alphabet Sampler.)

Gobelin Stem Stitch using 2-ply Persian. Back Stitch over 1 canvas thread. On 12-mesh.

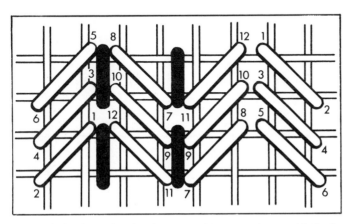

70. Gobelin Stem Stitch taken over 2 intersections, with Back Stitches taken over 2 canvas threads.

Leaf Stitch

Leaf Stitch may seem complicated at first to a beginner, but will appear quite simple after a few units are completed. Just follow diagram 71.

1. Start at the base of the leaf, coming out at 1 and going in at 2, stitching over 3 vertical and 4 horizontal canvas threads.

2. Come out at 3, in at 4, parallel to the first stitch.

3. Come out at 5, in at 6, again a parallel stitch.

4. Come out at 7 and go in at 8, which is 1 intersection in from 6.

5. Come out at 9 and go in at 10, which is another intersection in from 8, and come out at 11 and go in at 12.

6. Now come down the other side of the leaf, reversing the ins and outs, always coming out on the outside of the leaf and going in an occupied canvas opening.

7. Start the next leaf in line with the first, leaving 6 vertical canvas threads between the leaf bases (72).

8. After completing the leaves, work the straight stitch in a darker value or a different color. The next row is positioned so that the first stitch is taken 6 canvas threads below and 3 to the left or right of the row above. Several units of Leaf Stitch can be grouped in an arrangement (see letter T in the Alphabet Sampler). Rows in varying colors or values can make an allover pattern (see letter B), or a single row can be used as a border.

Leaf Stitch in shaded rows using 3-ply Persian; Straight Gobelin Stitch veins in 4-ply French silk. On 12-mesh.

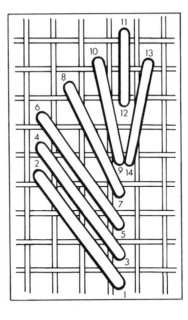

71. Half of the Leaf Stitch unit is worked from the base up, the other half from the top down.

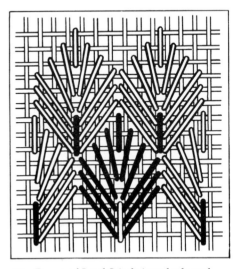

72. Rows of Leaf Stitch interlock and create a solid ground.

Leaf Stitch Medallion

Leaf Stitch Medallion is a motif composed of 4 perpendicular Leaf Stitch units radiating around a central mesh opening. Note that the individual stitches in the Leaf Stitch units have a different arrangement from those shown in diagram 71.

Complete 4 Leaf Stitch units as shown (73). Then work the 8 vein stitches that converge in the center open space. Use a contrasting value or color for accent. (See Leaf Stitch Medallion in section C3 of the Fan Sampler.)

Leaf Stitch Medallion and Tip of Leaf Stitch using 3-ply Nantucket Twist. On 13-mesh.

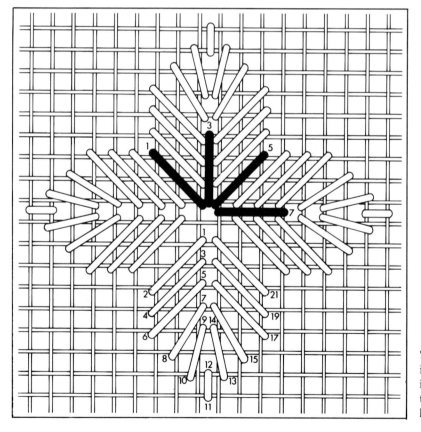

73. On one side of Leaf Stitch, individual stitches of the unit emerge in the center; on the opposite side they emerge at the edge of the leaf and enter the center.

71

Tip of Leaf Stitch

Tip of Leaf Stitch in both of the versions shown here is a useful background or border stitch. Start with the lowest Leaf Stitch and work stitches in pairs, 1 on the left, then 1 on the right, entering the straight stitch last. Use a contrasting thread for the 3 short stitches at the base of the leaf (74 and 75).

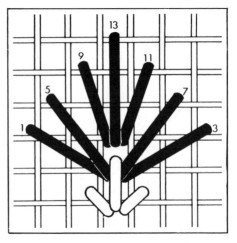

74. Each stitch of the Tip of Leaf unit emerges at the outer edge and is worked in a sequence of pairs.

75. This Tip of Leaf unit is only 5 canvas threads high and is worked in the same sequence as diagram 74.

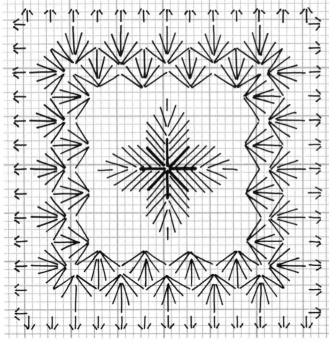

Note how the Tip of Leaf Stitch rows fit one into the other. The 3 small stitches at the base of the units are not shown on the graph for the sake of a clearer drawing.

Diagonal Leaf Stitch

Diagonal Leaf Stitch is a particularly welcome addition to the Leaf Stitch family. Use it when a slanted leaf pattern is needed.

Start all stitches of the unit at the outside of the leaf (76). Note the order in which you should take each stitch of the unit to have a centrally balanced placement of stitches. Work the vein stitch from upper left to lower right.

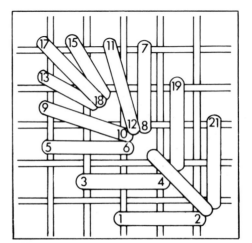

76. Follow the numbering sequence for stitch placement. Work the vein stitch last.

Diagonal Leaf Medallion

Diagonal Leaf Medallion is a motif composed of 4 Diagonal Leaf Stitch units sharing a center mesh opening (77).

Work each Leaf Stitch unit exactly as Diagonal Leaf Stitch (76). Use a contrasting color or value for the 4 diagonal stitches that act as veins for the leaves.

A Diagonal Leaf Medallion is expanded with added Diagonal Leaf Stitch units. The narrow border is created using just the tip of a leaf.

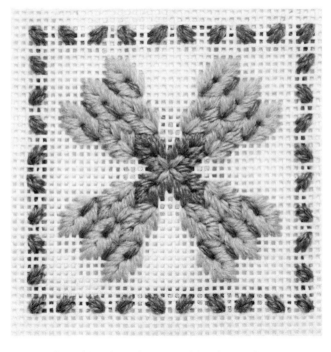

Diagonal Leaf Stitch and Diagonal Leaf Medallion, using 3-ply Nantucket Twist. On 13-mesh.

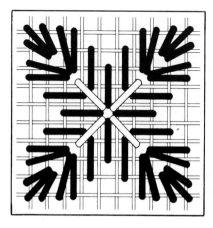

77. Work each segment as in 76. Turn the diagram or the work to follow the numbers.

Ray Stitch

Ray Stitch is a unit of 7 stitches that emerge from two sides of a square shape; all of them enter a common mesh opening in the corner.

Work these fanlike squares in alternate directions with each row (78), or all rows to fan out in the same direction, as in the graph for this stitch. Ray Stitch makes a handsome textured background. (See it in section H3 of the Fan Sampler.)

Ray and Diamond Ray Stitch using 2-ply Nantucket Twist. On 13-mesh.

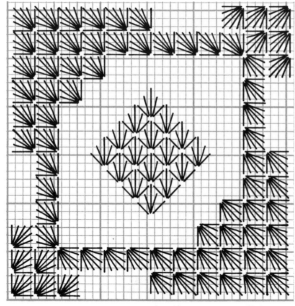

Center motif is a diamond shape of Diamond Ray Stitches. Border is composed of Ray Stitches radiating in various directions.

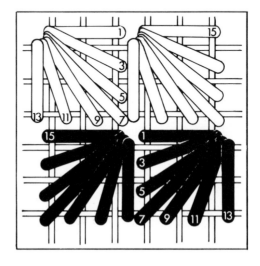

78. Work rows left to right when stitches fan out to the right. Work rows right to left when stitches fan to the left.

Diamond Ray Stitch

Diamond Ray Stitch is a unit of 5 stitches radiating out from the base of a diamond shape.

Work all stitches of the unit to emerge at the upper edges and enter a common mesh opening at the base; place them in a balanced arrangement (79). You may have to work the 2 outside stitches twice for good coverage. (See Diamond Ray in section B1 of the Fan Sampler.)

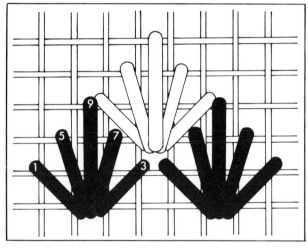

79. Work in horizontal rows, dropping down 2 canvas threads for each row.

Square Eyelet Stitch

Also called Algerian Eye or Eye Stitch

Small Square Eyelet Stitch units are composed of stitches taken over 2 canvas threads (80). For most Square Eyelets, every opening around the perimeter of the square is occupied (81). You may vary the size of the square but you must come out at the perimeter and enter the center opening for each stitch of the unit (82). Enlarge the center opening first with an awl or tapestry rug needle to make room for all the stitches that will converge around the center opening. Exert a pull as you come up at the perimeter to keep the center hole clear, but do not pull down after entering the perimeter, as this will pull the straight edge out of shape.

Square Eyelet makes handsome backgrounds. You can work a background in horizontal rows, stitching the top half as you travel from right to left and returning from left to right (83). You can also work diagonal rows, stitching the right side going up and the left side coming down (84). Use finer thread than usual to eliminate a high pile of stitches in the center. (See Square Eyelet in section D2 of the Fan Sampler.)

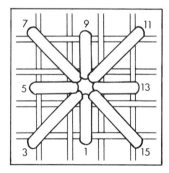

80. Small Square Eyelet uses 4 by 4 canvas threads, with all stitches entering the center opening.

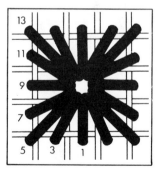

81. A small Square Eyelet uses all mesh holes around the perimeter.

(continued)

(Square Eyelet Stitch, *continued*)

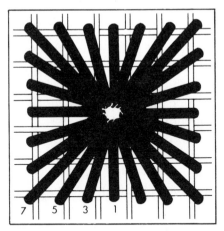

82. A large Square Eyelet may be any size, providing all stitches can enter the center opening and still keep it clear and neat.

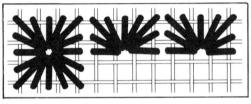

83. Square Eyelets worked in a horizontal row. The top half is worked first.

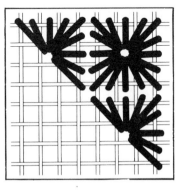

84. Square Eyelets worked in a diagonal row. The right half is worked first.

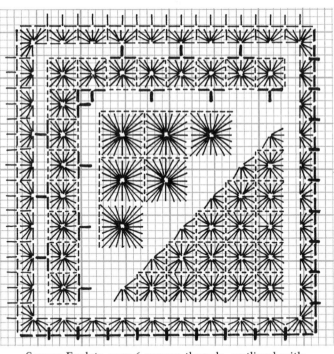

Square Eyelets over 6 canvas threads, outlined with Back Stitch over 1 canvas thread, share the center with Square Eyelets over 4 canvas threads. All are worked in diagonal rows. Half Square Eyelets frame the swatch.

Square Eyelet and Diamond Eyelet on Tent Stitch ground using 2-ply Persian. Shiny rayon for center Diamond Eyelet and for Back Stitch around squares. On 12-mesh.

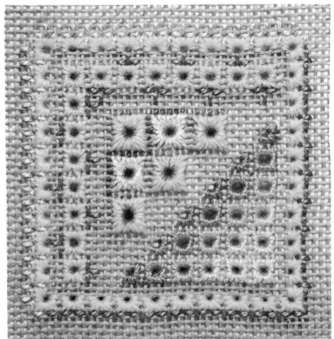

Square Eyelet using 1-ply Persian and size 5 pearl cotton; Half Square Eyelet in 2-ply Nantucket Twist; Back Stitch in size 5 pearl cotton. On tan 13-mesh.

Diamond Eyelet Stitch

Also called Diamond Star Stitch

Diamond Eyelet is another dramatic Eyelet Stitch.

When using more than one unit, be sure to work each one of them passing in the same direction, clockwise or counter-clockwise, starting with a vertical stitch at the bottom (85). As any Eyelet Stitch is worked, each stitch in the unit should enter the center opening. Fasten off each time by snugly passing the thread through the stitches on the back around the center opening. You can elaborate on a Diamond Eyelet with a thin contrasting thread: Overstitch the vertical and horizontal stitches and take 4 long stitches from what would be the square corners all into the center opening (86). (The Diamond Eyelet is used in letter B of the Alphabet Sampler and in the Square Eyelet Stitch swatch.)

Diamond Eyelet and half Diamond Eyelet in 2-ply Persian, long stitch accents on 2 Diamond Eyelets in 1-ply Persian, Tent Stitch accents, in size 5 pearl cotton. On 13-mesh.

A solid area of Diamond Eyelet is worked in diagonal rows as shown in diagram 84 for Square Eyelet, working the right side going up the row and the left side coming down. Two sizes of Diamond Eyelet are worked in the remaining field of canvas. Half Diamonds make a handsome border.

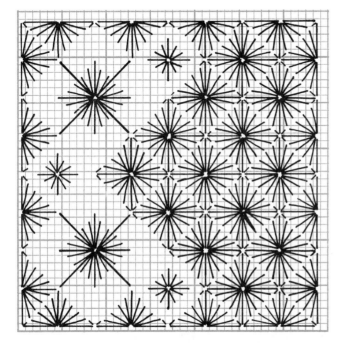

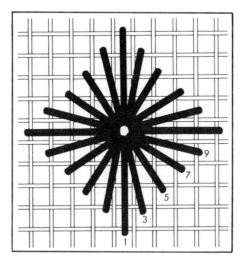

85. Every mesh opening around the diamond shape perimeter is used; all stitches of the unit enter the center opening.

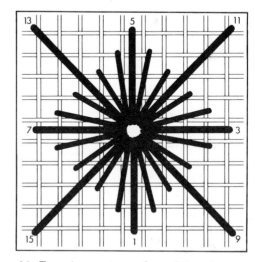

86. Two sizes or two colors of thread are used to create more drama. Work the Diamond Eyelet first, then overstitch with a second thread.

77

Round Eyelet Stitch

Round Eyelet differs from Square Eyelet in that there are short diagonal stitches in place of the long corner stitches (87). Use half Round Eyelet to make handsome edgings; work it in horizontal rows (88). For a Round Eyelet background, work half Round Eyelet in horizontal or diagonal rows and complete it with a return journey. If Round Eyelet is worked one under the other, Diamond Eyelet will fill the remaining open canvas. (See the graph on this page. See Round and Diamond Eyelet filling in sections C1 and F5 of the Fan Sampler.)

Irregular Eyelet

Irregular Eyelet is useful to break up the rigid geometry of a needlepoint design. You may work it freely with the stitches of each unit converging in an opening that is off center (89).

Irregular Eyelet can have perimeters of any shape; it can be oval, part round, part square, but they must have a pronounced opening where the stitches enter. You can also plan it on graph paper to have a pleasing shape. It is most effective when the units dovetail one into the other, using many colors and values to highlight the irregular shapes.

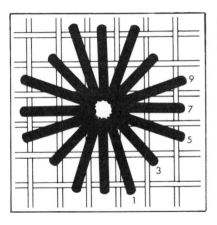

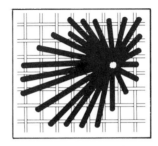

87. Travel around the perimeter, entering the center opening with each stitch.

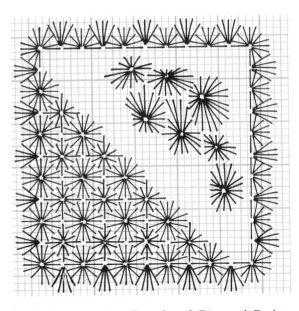

89. Irregular Eyelets have an off-center opening and all stitches regardless of length must enter there.

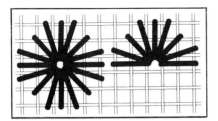

88. Work Half Round Eyelets in a horizontal row. To fill a solid area, complete the Eyelets with a return journey and continue to work in horizontal rows.

In the lower section Round and Diamond Eyelets make a solid ground. Irregular Eyelets make another ground in the upper section. Half and quarter Eyelets frame the top and side.

Round, Half Round, and Irregular Eyelet Stitches, using 2-ply Nantucket and size 5 pearl cotton. On 13-mesh.

Straight Stitches

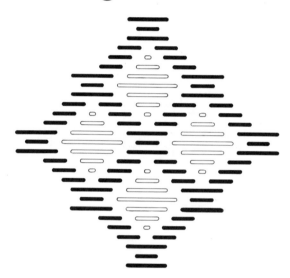

Back Stitch
Outline Back Stitch
Oblique Back Stitch
Whipped Back Stitch
Threaded Back Stitch
Crewel Stem Stitch
Outline Stem Stitch
Alternating Stem Stitch
Overstitched Back Stitch
Running Stitch
Double Running Stitch
Darning
Bucky's Weaving
Sashiko Quilting on Canvas
Kogin
Straight Gobelin Stitch
False Gobelin Stitch
Tramé
Brick Stitch
Parisian Stitch
Hungarian Stitch
Hungarian Diamond
Triangle Stitch
Florentine Embroidery
   Florentine Stitch
   Bargello

Back Stitch

Many know Back Stitch from experience with hand sewing. Back Stitch is used for outlines and backgrounds. It is made by drawing the needle through the canvas from the far end of the stitch and coming to the front end to close it. Back Stitch makes long stitches on the back of the work and short ones on the front. Remember, in looking over the diagrams, odd numbers come out to the front of the canvas and even numbers go down through the canvas. Back Stitch is a big thread-eater and makes a thick mat on the back of the canvas when used for a solid background.

Back Stitch can be worked over any reasonable number of mesh. Diagrams 90 and 91 show different methods for turning a corner. Use it over 1 or 2 canvas threads between rows of other stitches for added embellishment, or to cover unwanted grin-through of canvas (92). Back Stitch is often used around

Eyelet Stitch for these reasons. When Back Stitch is used to cover a solid area of canvas, it has the appearance of an old tapestry. Stagger the stitches in brick formation for better coverage on a single mesh (93). Use all horizontal canvas openings on a double mesh, but do not split the vertical ones (94). Work Back Stitch with a light tension so that the canvas lies flat without buckling.

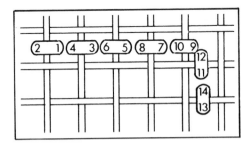

90. Back Stitch worked over a single canvas thread. Note how corner is turned.

Back Stitch using 2-ply Persian to produce a heavy ribbed look. On 11 double mesh, but 10 would work equally well and is more readily available.

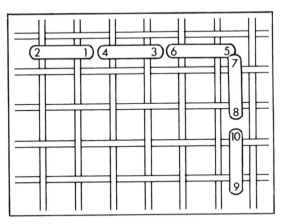

91. Back Stitch worked over 2 canvas threads. Note corner is turned in a sequence of stitches that avoids a slanted stitch on the back that might show in an open canvas design.

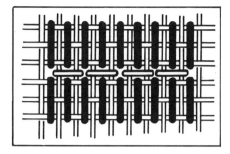

92. Back Stitch worked over 2 canvas threads to cover grin-through between rows of Straight Gobelin Stitch.

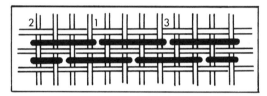

93. Back Stitch used for solid areas shown worked here over 4 canvas threads, staggered brick fashion for better coverage.

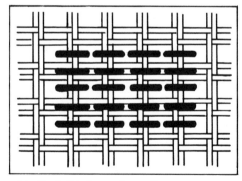

94. Back Stitch works well on double mesh over closely woven vertical threads and between rows of open horizontal threads, resulting in a handsome ribbed effect.

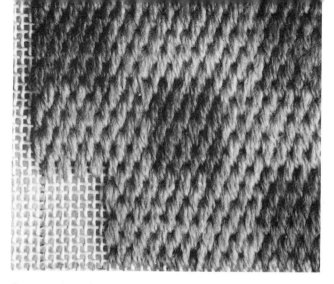

Staggered Back Stitch over 4 horizontal canvas threads. Checkered effect created with two values of same color, using 3-ply Persian. On 12-mesh.

Bands of Back Stitch worked in two directions: Horizontal bands stitched horizontally and verticals, vertically. Open squares filled with Straight Gobelin Stitch, using 3-ply Persian. On 14-mesh.

Outline Back Stitch, Oblique Back Stitch

Outline Back Stitch and Oblique Back Stitch are valuable aids in laying out a design in a reversible way. The stitches can easily be ripped without leaving a permanent marking on the canvas.

With fine thread, such as sewing cotton, Back Stitch over 2 canvas threads to outline a design. You can stitch over this later. To outline effectively note that you can work Back Stitch in oblique directions as well as horizontally, vertically, and diagonally. Work Oblique Back Stitch over 2 horizontal and 1 vertical, or over 1 horizontal and 2 vertical canvas threads (95). It is possible to work circles (96) and rounded shapes of any kind (97). Back Stitch over the fine planning stitches, or plunge in from the start with the desired weight of thread.

Whipped and Threaded Back Stitch, using matte cotton and size 5 pearl cotton. On 14-mesh.

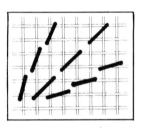

95. Back Stitch worked over intersections to produce three different angles:

Over 2 horizontals and 1 vertical
Over 2 horizontals and 2 verticals
Over 1 horizontal and 2 verticals

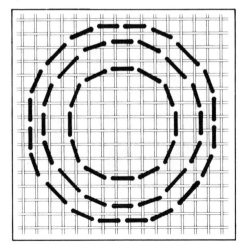

96. Backstitch perfect circles using some oblique stitches.

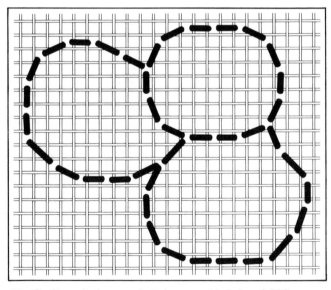

97. Outline nicely rounded shapes with help of Oblique Back Stitch.

Whipped Back Stitch

Whipped Back Stitch is an overcast Back Stitch that produces a fine, smooth line. Work Back Stitch first with moderate tension so that the needle can easily pass under the stitches. Enter the canvas only to emerge and to fasten off. Come to the front at the base of a Back Stitch, pass the needle over the next Back Stitch, then slide the needle under it from the top (98). Use Whipped Back Stitch to achieve smooth, curving lines. (See Whipped Back Stitch on flower design of Sashiko Quilted Vest.)

Threaded Back Stitch

Threaded Back Stitch is Back Stitch embellished with a heavier, contrasting thread that passes under 2 stitches and over 2 stitches (99). Work the Back Stitch first with only moderate tension so that the needle can slide under the stitches easily. Enter the canvas only to emerge and to fasten off.

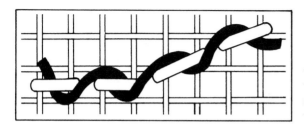

98. Whip Back Stitch with an overcast stitch to produce a thin, smooth line.

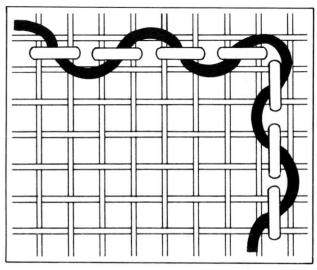

99. Thread a Back Stitch with heavier thread to produce a raised, textured line.

Back Stitch is used for the small alphabet and number series. Whipped Back Stitch is used for graceful script to resemble your own handwriting. Threaded Back Stitch is used for a fine decorative raised border.

Crewel Stem Stitch

Stem Stitch is what appears on the underside of the canvas when working Back Stitch. There are three ways to Stem Stitch; they differ only in whether the thread is held above or below the needle.

Work Crewel Stem Stitch from left to right, holding the thread below the needle. Point the needle away from the direction of the row, advance over 4 canvas threads, and retreat under 2. This is a practical-size stitch and is the size used in this book. You can, however, take stitches of any length and vary them as you stitch. Stitch between the rows of canvas threads (100) or over them (101). Crewel Stem produces a rough-textured line, Outline Stem a smoother finer line.

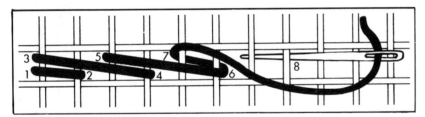

100. Crewel Stem Stitch moves forward over 4 canvas threads and back 2 between 2 rows of canvas threads. Working thread is held under the needle.

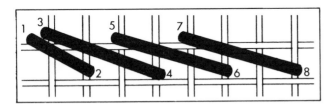

101. Crewel Stem Stitch moves forward over 4 and back 2 while covering a horizontal thread.

Outline Stem Stitch

Work Outline Stem Stitch from left to right holding the thread above the needle. Point the needle away from the row, advance over 4 canvas threads, and retreat under 2 (102 and 103). Outline and Crewel Stem can be worked right to left, but you must reverse the position of the thread in relation to the needle. You can produce a subtly shaded background with long Outline or Crewel Stem. Stagger the length of the rows with each color so that colors or values blend (104).

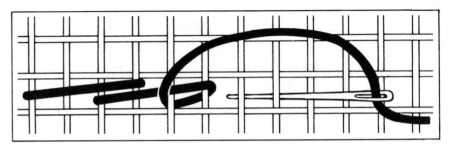

102. Outline Stem moves forward over 4 and back 2 between 2 rows of canvas thread. Working thread is held over the needle.

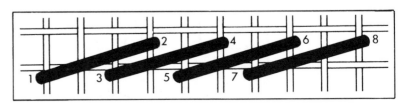

103. Outline Stem moves forward 4 and back 2 while covering a horizontal canvas thread.

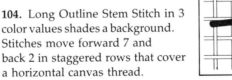

104. Long Outline Stem Stitch in 3 color values shades a background. Stitches move forward 7 and back 2 in staggered rows that cover a horizontal canvas thread.

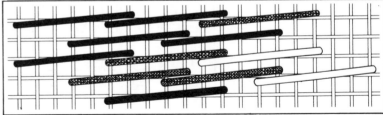

Alternating Stem Stitch

Work Alternating Stem Stitch holding the thread above the needle for one stitch and below for the next. This produces a double row of stitches (105). Alternating Stem Stitch is very useful when you want to add a simple outline around a design with a minimum of effort.

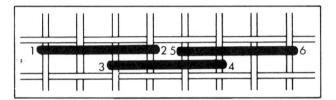

105. Alternating Stem is stitched with the working thread held first above and then below the needle for each stitch.

Crewel, Outline, Alternating Stem Stitch, using Brilliant Embroidery and Cutwork Thread, and matte cotton. On 13-mesh.

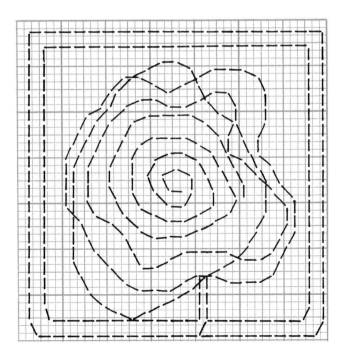

A flower is freely worked in Back Stitch, then overstitched in Stem Stitch.

Overstitched Back Stitch

It is far easier to work a graceful outline on canvas with Back Stitch than it is with Stem Stitch. First work Back Stitch with a fine thread in a matching color (106). Then add weight and texture with Stem Stitch worked over the Back Stitch. Pass forward over 2 and back under 1 Back Stitch (107).

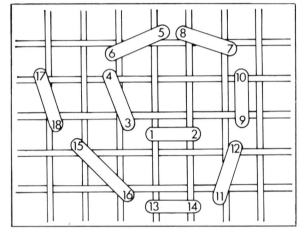

106. Backstitch a curved shape first.

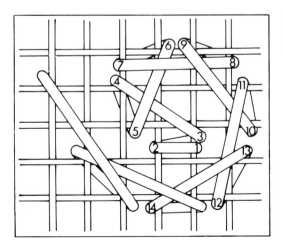

107. Stemstitch over the Back Stitch; note the sequence of numbers.

Running Stitch

Running Stitch is certainly a familiar stitch to a hand sewer. A convenient-size stitch for most canvas mesh moves forward over 2 and under 2 (108). Running Stitch can travel in any direction (see the oblique directions in which Back Stitch can travel). When Running Stitch is used, much of the canvas is left open. Since starting and ending is difficult when there is no solid area to hide behind, use a working thread that is twice as long as usual. Let half the thread dangle and travel in one direction, then thread the needle with the other half and travel in the opposite direction. Also use this method with the darning techniques that follow. If you have no worked area in which to start or fasten off, take a Back Stitch over 1 canvas thread in each direction under a Running Stitch.

Double Running Stitch

Double Running Stitch is Running Stitch worked with a return journey that fills the vacant mesh (108). Use Double Running on a fine mesh, leaving much of the canvas open and unworked to capture the look of old Blackwork. Authentic Double Running Stitch looks exactly the same on both sides of the work (109).

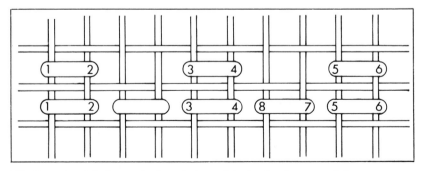

108. Running Stitch travels from left to right in the first row; it becomes Double Running Stitch in the second row with the working of a return journey.

Monogrammed Elizabethan strapwork design, using size 5 pearl cotton. On linen canvas, 17-mesh.

Back Stitch is used in the center. To work it in Double Running would require a great deal of time to plan the journeys on a graph using arrows. You might enjoy the challenge. Double Running is used for the reversible borders. Enter your own monogram.

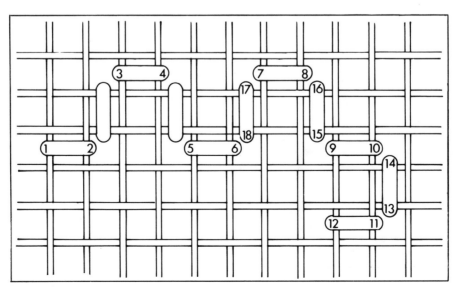

109. Double Running Stitch in a reversible "battlement" design. Study the number sequence to see how this reversible pattern is worked.

Darning

Darning is a Running Stitch worked in an allover pattern as a filling stitch. The canvas itself becomes an integrated part of the pattern. Use this simple Darning pattern for a richly woven fabric background.

Work the first set of Running Stitch in one fiber, with 4 canvas threads between the horizontal rows (110). Then enter a second set in a second fiber centered between the first set (111). Give the canvas a quarter turn and enter the third and fourth fibers. (See the graph.) Use long working threads divided in half, as described for Running Stitch.

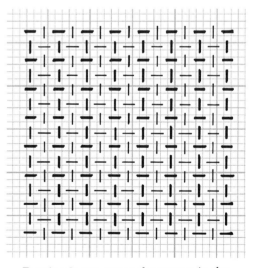

Darning pattern using white Cairo cotton and off-white Nantucket Twist in the vertical rows, white Bunka and white linen thread in the horizontal rows. On 13-mesh.

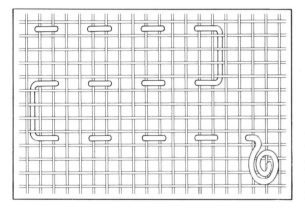

110. Enter the first row of stitches. Use a long working thread. Let half the thread dangle, work the area above, and then work below with remaining thread.

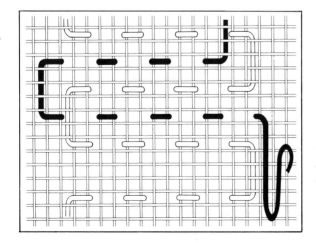

111. Enter a second set of stitches centered between the first rows. This can be the same fiber or a new one.

Darning incorporates the canvas in the pattern.

88

Bucky's Weaving

Bucky's Weaving combines Darning with Cross Stitch.

Work the Cross Stitch first, over 2 by 2 canvas threads, skipping 1 canvas thread on all sides. (See Cross Stitch.) Work the Darning pattern with pairs of parallel Running Stitch over 5 canvas threads. Complete the vertical Darning, turn the canvas, and work the horizontal Darning (112). Use tightly twisted silk or cotton floss for the Darning, and the same thread laid flat for the Cross Stitch. (See Bucky's Weaving in Flower Pictures I and II.)

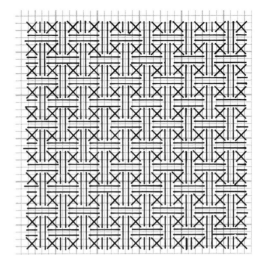

This darning pattern, worked in two directions with shiny thread reflecting light, is also called Damask Darning.

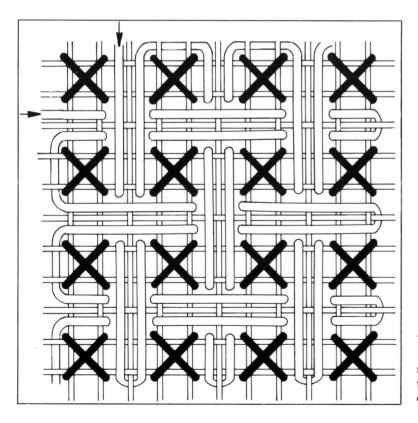

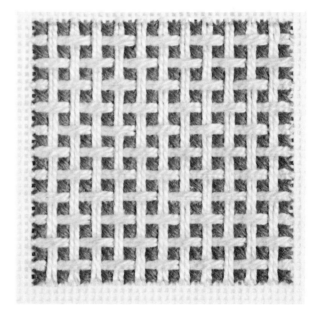

Bucky's Weaving, using size 3 pearl cotton for Darning, 3-ply Nantucket Twist for Cross Stitch. On 13-mesh.

112. Work the Cross Stitch first to set the pattern. Darn the pairs of horizontal stitches, turn the canvas, and darn the vertical stitches. Note the short compensating stitches at the edges.

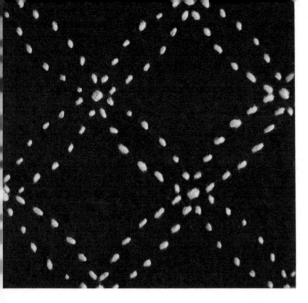

This swatch shows the fabric side of Sashiko Quilting on canvas. The pattern of Connecting Circles is one of a large selection of traditional Sashiko designs, each with its own pathways. See a larger graph for this pattern with Sashiko Vest instructions in Projects section.

Sashiko Quilting on Canvas

Sashiko Quilting is an eighteenth-century Japanese folk technique, originally sewn through one or two cotton indigo-dyed fabrics sewn together with soft white cotton in Running Stitch patterns. Sashiko Quilting has grown from a technique designed to provide warmth and long wear into one of today's textile arts.

Old Sashiko was not a counted thread technique but now, with canvas as the top surface, you can easily achieve even Running Stitch patterns on both faces of the fabric. To work Sashiko Quilting on canvas, try tan canvas, coarse black cotton backing, working threads of matte cotton and Brilliant Embroidery and Cutwork Thread, and a crewel or chenille needle. The work is completely reversible (if care is taken with starting and ending). To work a small piece, baste the two fabrics together and stretch them on a frame. Use a stabbing method to stitch. Pass over 2 canvas threads or 2 intersections and under 1 canvas thread or 1 intersection for each Running Stitch to work this particular Connected Circles pattern (113). Other patterns may

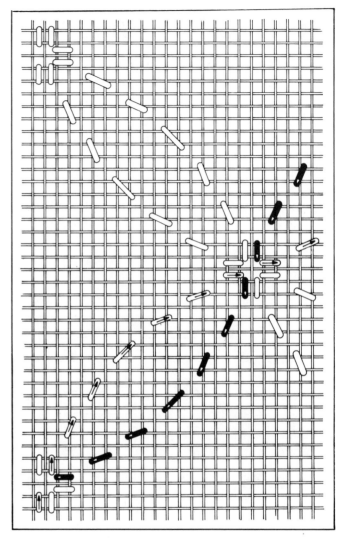

113. Start with 2 straight vertical Running Stitches. Note there is one intersection between them and all the other stitches. The vertical stitches gradually change their direction to become horizontal stitches.

be worked over 2 and under 2. For a large piece, such as a vest or jacket, consult the Projects section for the Sashiko Quilted Reversible Vest. There you will also see photographs of both sides of the work and some other Sashiko patterns.

Kogin

Kogin (pronounced Ko GEEN) is an old Japanese folk embroidery. Traditionally worked on coarse, even-weave, indigo-dyed linen with soft white cotton thread, Kogin was used to reinforce work clothing. Now, like Sashiko, it too has become a textile art. Work Kogin patterns with stitches in varying lengths in horizontal rows (114 and 115). A reverse pattern develops on the back, which makes Kogin suitable for working a reversible garment. Canvas is an ideal fabric for Kogin. Use very long thread to complete long rows and to avoid frequent need to fasten off and on. When working on unlined canvas try to start and end threads in margins. When working Kogin through two fabrics secure thread between the two layers. (See Kogin on the Sashiko Quilted Vest.)

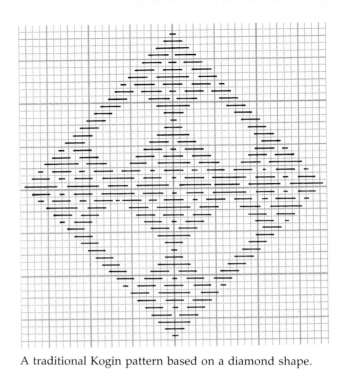

A traditional Kogin pattern based on a diamond shape.

Kogin pattern, using lightly twisted white 6-ply embroidery floss. On 14-mesh, painted with blue Deka dye.

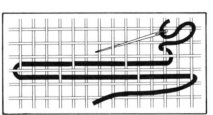

114. Kogin darning worked in horizontal rows. Note how the thread is passed from one row to the other.

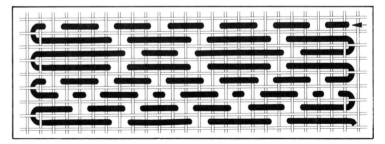

115. Vary the length of the stitches within each row and in neighboring rows to create a pattern. This is the same pattern seen in section G3 of the Fan Sampler and also on the yoke of the Sashiko Quilted Vest in the Projects section.

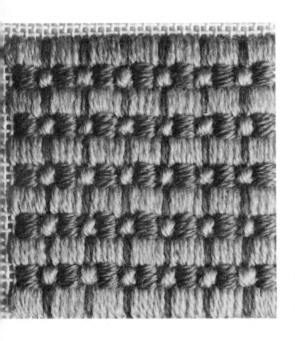

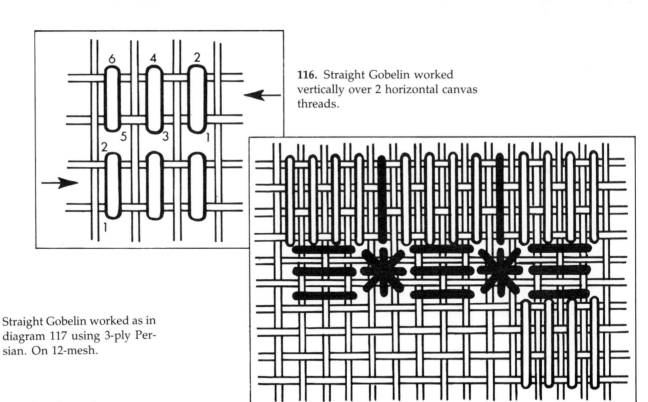

116. Straight Gobelin worked vertically over 2 horizontal canvas threads.

Straight Gobelin worked as in diagram 117 using 3-ply Persian. On 12-mesh.

117. Straight Gobelin worked vertically in one row and horizontally in the next where it alternates with Smyrna Stitch (see Cross Stitch section).

Straight Gobelin Stitch

Also called Satin Stitch and Upright Gobelin Stitch

Straight Gobelin is one of the easiest stitches. It is worked vertically or horizontally over 2, 3, 4, or more canvas threads. Work alternate rows in alternate directions: left to right, then right to left. Start each stitch by emerging at the base and entering the canvas at the top of the stitch (116). Turn canvas to work horizontal stitches (117).

Since these straight stitches do not interlock one row into the next, exposed canvas may grin through between the rows. Maintain an even, loose tension and use a full strand of thread to minimize this. Back Stitch in matching lighter-weight thread can be worked between the rows to cover grin-through.

Because Straight Gobelin can be worked in 2 directions it becomes a good choice for borders. If a padded look is desired, a Tramé thread can be laid first (see Tramé in this section). Straight Gobelin combines well with other stitches.

Corner of border made by reversing direction of stitches, using 3-ply Persian. On 12-mesh. (See this swatch fully worked with initial and date in Patchwork Sampler I.)

92

False Gobelin Stitch

False Gobelin Stitch is useful for creating textured bands with nubbly or piled threads like chenille that you can manage only with care to feed through the eye of a needle or maneuver in and out of the canvas. Use only threads that are heavier in girth than the threads of the canvas itself.

Emerge at the base of the stitch and enter the top; emerge at the top and enter the base of the next stitch (118). (See the chenille borders on Flower Pictures I and II.)

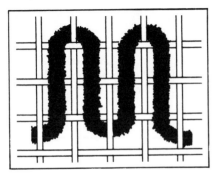

118. False Gobelin over 3 canvas threads.

Tramé, with 2-ply Persian under Straight Gobelin using 3-ply.
Tramé, with 1-ply Persian under Half Cross using 2-ply. On 10 double mesh.

Tramé

Also called Tram

Tramé is a very useful method for padding both diagonal and straight stitches, not only for better coverage of the canvas, but for a raised effect (119 and 120). Traditionally it refers to a laid horizontal thread, usually wool, on painted double-mesh canvas. The tramé indicates the color yarn to use. It also fills out the Half Cross Stitch to be worked over it.

To work Tramé, use the same thread as for stitching, but 1 ply fewer. Take long irregular-length Running Stitch, passing under 1 canvas thread between the long stitches.

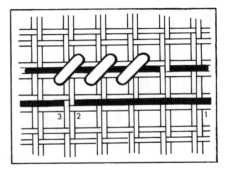

119. Tramé under Half Cross on double mesh.

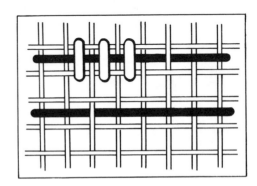

120. Tramé under Straight Gobelin on single mesh.

93

Brick Stitch

Brick Stitch is not a single stitch but a series of Straight Gobelin Stitch taken over 2 or 4 canvas threads laid in staggered rows like bricks.

Work Brick Stitch vertically or horizontally (121 and 122). Work the vertical stitches in horizontal rows, alternating them from left to right and right to left. Work the horizontal stitches in vertical rows alternating from top down and bottom up. Skip a space between each stitch in the first row. Enter this space in the second row, interlocking the rows. Enter compensating stitches by anticipating them or fill them in afterward. Brick Stitch is an excellent background stitch and is a good choice for shading and blending colors.

Horizontal Brick Stitch over 4 vertical canvas threads blended for a skylike effect. At lower edge, shaded Brick Stitch worked over 2 horizontal canvas threads, using 3-ply Persian. On 12-mesh.

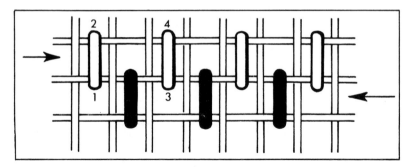

121. Vertical Brick Stitch over 2 horizontal canvas threads.

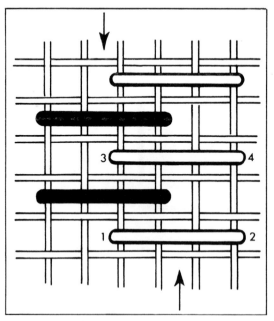

122. Horizontal Brick Stitch over 4 vertical canvas threads.

Parisian Stitch

Parisian Stitch is not a single stitch but a series of alternating long and short stitches laid in rows. The stitches also alternate long under short and short under long.

In the first row, work the stitches horizontally or vertically over a series of 4 and 2 or 3 and 1 canvas threads (123, 124, and 125). In the second row fit a short stitch under a long and a long stitch under a short. Alternate these two rows, working from right to left and left to right, or from the top down and the bottom up.

There are many ways to vary Parisian Stitch. Try working all short stitches first in one thread, long ones later in another. Or try working different combinations of long and short stitches (126 and 127). (See Parisian Stitch in section C3 of Fan Sampler.)

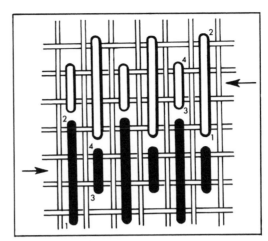

123. Parisian Stitch worked over 4 and 2 horizontal canvas threads. Note long stitch under short and short under long.

In center Parisian Stitch in 2 colors worked over 4 and 2 canvas threads. Parisian over 3 and 1 vertical canvas threads surround it. Outermost band is Straight Gobelin with Flat Stitch corners, using 3-ply Persian. On 14-mesh.

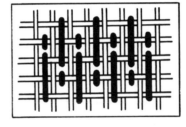

124. Parisian Stitch worked over 3 and 1 horizontal canvas threads.

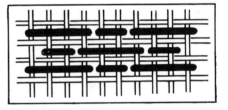

125. Parisian Stitch worked over 4 and 2 vertical canvas threads.

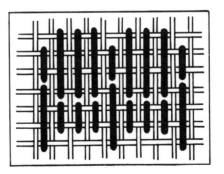

126. Parisian Stitch variation.

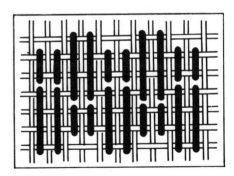

127. Parisian Stitch variation.

Hungarian Stitch

Hungarian Stitch is a unit of straight stitches progressing in size from small to large to small. Hungarian Stitch travels across a row leaving space between each unit for the subsequent row to enter.

Work the first stitch of a unit over 2 canvas threads, the second over 4, the last stitch of the unit as the first. Stitch the rows in alternate directions, from left to right, then right to left. Placement of the second row may be confusing. The thing to remember is, the space to be skipped in the second row is one directly under the long stitch in the row above. Once you have completed the second row, the others will fall into place. Take stitches into the space of the preceding row, short stitches under short and long under long; every other row is identical (128).

There are many variations of Hungarian Stitch. In diagram 129, 2 stitches of each length are worked creating a chainlike repeat. (See Hungarian Stitch in section C4 of Fan Sampler.)

Wave Stitch rows (see Bargello in this section) filled with Hungarian Stitch; a pattern known as Hungarian Ground, using 3-ply Persian. On 12-mesh.

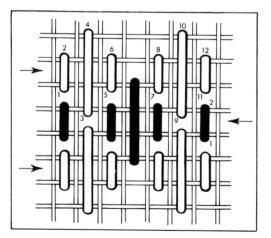

128. Hungarian Stitch in horizontal rows. The long stitches in the second row, shown in black, enter spaces in the first row.

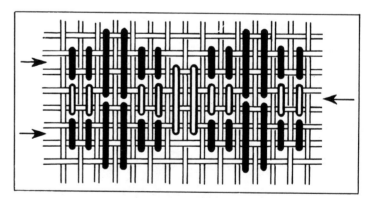

129. Hungarian variation; each unit is composed of 6 stitches worked over 2, 2, 4, 4, 2, 2 canvas threads. A space is skipped between the units. Note the third row is the same as first.

Hungarian Diamond

Hungarian Diamond is one of many Hungarian Stitch variations. Each unit is composed of 5 or 7 stitches taken over 2, 4, 6, 4, 2 or 2, 4, 6, 8, 6, 4, 2 canvas threads (130).

Work rows in alternate directions from right to left and left to right. To work Hungarian Diamond on its side, give the canvas a quarter turn. Hungarian Diamond combines well with Hungarian Stitch and with Wave Stitch as shown in the accompanying swatches.

Hungarian, Hungarian Diamond, Tent, and Wave Stitch combined in handsome repeat pattern, using 3-ply Persian. On 12-mesh.

In very center, 4 Hungarian Stitches slanting in 2 directions occupy the same center mesh opening. Vertical Hungarian Diamonds surround center. Hungarian Stitch background worked horizontally. Half Hungarian Diamonds along 2 sides, using 3-ply Persian. On 14-mesh.

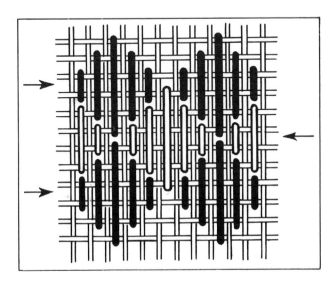

130. Each unit is composed of stitches taken over 2, 4, 6, 4, 2. In the second row the long stitch enters the skipped space in the first row. Every other row is alike.

97

Triangle Stitch

Triangle Stitch is a composite stitch consisting of 4 triangular units, each one being half of a Hungarian Diamond. All 4 units share a center mesh opening and they occupy a square of 10 canvas threads.

Work the first stitch of a triangle over 2 horizontal canvas threads, the remaining over 3, 4, 5, 4, 3, 2. Give the canvas a quarter turn to work the horizontal triangles. After completing all 4 triangles, enter the compensating stitches in the corners. Corners can be filled with small Cross Stitch as in 131, Smyrna Stitch as in letter V of the Alphabet Sampler, or Mosaic Stitch as shown in an accompanying swatch. (See Triangle Stitch in section I3 of Fan Sampler.)

Triangle Stitch ground with 4 Mosaic Stitches worked at intersections, each one pointing toward center mesh opening. Back Stitch over 5 canvas threads entered last. Using 3-ply Persian. On 14-mesh.

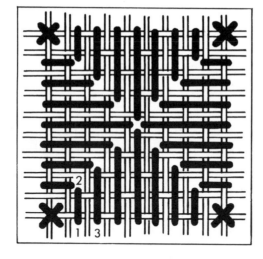

131. Four half Hungarian Diamonds share a center mesh opening. Corners can be filled with Cross Stitch, Smyrna, or Mosaic.

Triangle Stitch in center sets direction of all stitches in swatch: 2 rows Straight Gobelin outlined with Back Stitch, 2 rows interlocking triangles. Note mitered corners. Using 3-ply Persian for Triangle Stitch, all else in 2-ply. On 14-mesh.

Florentine Embroidery

Florentine Embroidery is the name given to a specialized form of canvas embroidery characterized by straight stitches of regulated length that rhythmically rise and fall to form zigzag designs.

Many Florentine patterns call for blocks of equal-size stitches in a straight line. Stitch this type of pattern with a fuller thread and with looser tension. When the looser stitches are pressed down with blocking and steaming they will cover the exposed canvas threads.

Use tan 13-mesh canvas with 3-ply Persian or 4-ply Nantucket Twist to get started. Later try smaller mesh for finer results, and experiment with various threads. If you are unsure of the amount of thread to use for a particular canvas, work a sample swatch to test various weights.

All stitches in Florentine Embroidery emerge at the base and go in at the top. When descending from a peak, a long stitch is made on the back of the canvas; when ascending, a short stitch is made. Work rows in alternate directions so that the back of the canvas gets an even distribution of thread. This will give your work a flatter appearance.

Since Florentine Embroidery is done by counting, a type of shorthand is sometimes used. The number of canvas threads that a stitch covers is given first, then the number of canvas threads, or steps, that it rises or falls. Example: 4.2 step means that the stitches are taken over 4 canvas threads and each is begun 2 canvas threads above the last.

Florentine Embroidery with classic carnation motif, using 2-ply Persian for outline, 7-ply French silk for filling. On white 10 double mesh.

Florentine Stitch

Also called Irish Stitch and Flame Stitch

Florentine Stitch is a style of Florentine Embroidery in which all the stitches are the same size. Generally they are taken over 4 horizontal threads and they rise and fall 2 steps.

The carnation swatch is a typical Florentine Stitch flower design in a 4.2 step. Most of these old designs are easy to follow from examples to be found in the textile department of a museum or in a local historical society.

The mille fleur design is a little repeat pattern of my own invention suitable for small or delicate items. Both of these swatches are worked on white 10 double mesh. This is a thinner fabric than single-mesh canvas and is easier to make up into accessories. The canvas is held so that the closely woven threads are in a horizontal position, the selvages at the top and bottom. By using all the spaces between the now vertical threads, and counting the double threads as 2, a petit point Florentine Stitch is made (132). (See the mille fleur pattern in color in Patchwork Sampler I.)

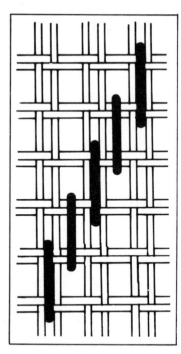

132. Florentine Stitch on double mesh, taken over 2 pairs of closely woven canvas threads, rising or falling 1 pair, a 4.2 step. Stitches are taken between all vertical canvas threads.

Mille fleur design on single mesh. See description on this page to work double mesh. All threads are Persian except for background, which is white silk, and Upright Cross at trellis intersections, which is yellow silk.

100

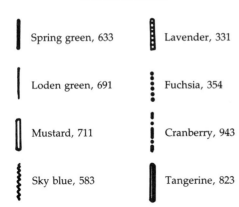

Spring green, 633

Loden green, 691

Mustard, 711

Sky blue, 583

Lavender, 331

Fuchsia, 354

Cranberry, 943

Tangerine, 823

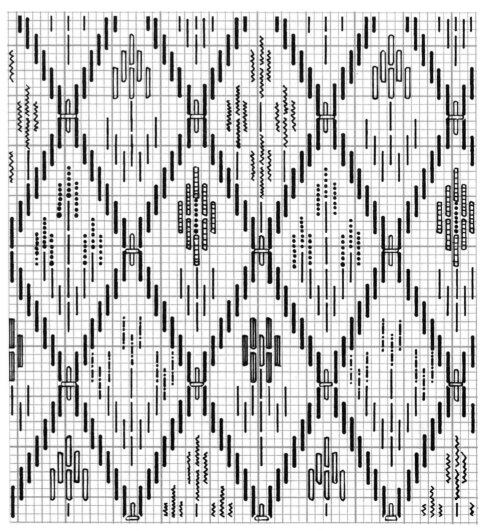

Florentine Embroidery with flower and trellis design using 2-ply Persian. Background and Upright Cross Stitch at intersections using 7-ply French silk. On white 10 double mesh. Selvages held top and bottom.

Bargello

Bargello is another style of Florentine Embroidery. It is characterized by long stitches regularly interspersed with shorter ones. The steps between the stitches can vary. Bargello has come to be a generic term used by many for all patterns composed of straight stitches. Very old Bargello patterns can be recognized by the use of very long and very short stitches with a secondary pattern made by the short stitches. (See the graph and swatch on the following page, also in color in Patchwork Sampler I, and section F2 of Fan Sampler.)

A wave pattern is the simplest Bargello design (133). Rise 1 step with each stitch; work 4 ascending stitches, then 4 descending (count the first and last stitch each time). In the next row, stitch over 2 canvas threads rising and falling 1 step.

To round a wave, work a block of stitches at the crest and at the base of the wave (134). In this diagram blocks are worked with 3 stitches over 4 canvas threads in one row and 3 stitches over 3 in the next row.

The antique Bargello flame pattern consists of 1 long stitch and 4 short ones in steps of 1. The long stitch is over 6 canvas threads and the short one over 2. The stitch pattern is established in the first row and is repeated after working 4 more rows. Note the pattern consists of 1 long and 4 short stitches both horizontally and vertically.

To set up a Bargello, center the stitch in the first row of the repeat in the center of the canvas. Work from the center to the left and then to the right in order to place the pattern evenly across the canvas. All other rows start alternately right and left. Center a design vertically by starting in the center, work down from the center, then turn the canvas and work the other half.

Wave pattern as in diagram 133. Diamond shape openings achieved by reversing direction of waves in center. Hungarian Diamond and Diamond Eyelet fill wave openings. Using 3-ply Persian. Narrow waves using size 3 pearl cotton. On 14-mesh.

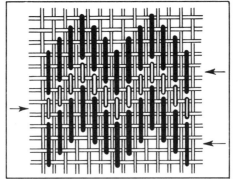

133. Rows of waves are worked in alternate directions. When all rows are worked in the same direction, concentration of thick and thin stitches form on the back and create pleats.

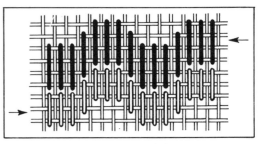

134. Blocks of stitches round the waves.

Pattern composed of 1 long stitch over 6 and 4 short stitches over 2. Note that the vertical repeat is also the same, 1 long and 4 short stitches. Turn the graph upside down to start with the bottom row. Work the stitches emerging at the base and going in at the top. Start the first row by centering the pattern.

Formal and elegant old Bargello flame pattern using 5-ply French silk and 2-ply Nantucket Twist. On 24-mesh. (See this pattern in section F2 of Fan Sampler.)

Cross Stitches

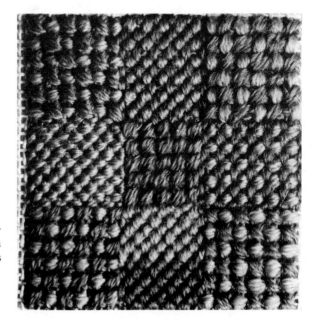

Center square is Cross Stitch. Other squares use variations of Upright Cross and diagonal Cross Stitch (diagrams 135–145). All stitches over 2 by 2 canvas threads, using 3-ply Persian. On 12-mesh.

Cross Stitch

Also called Gros Point

Cross Stitch is a unit of 2 Half Cross Stitch. The first cross slants from lower right to upper left and the second from lower left to upper right (135). Cross the stitches in this order to blend with Tent Stitch. If you are not using Tent Stitch you can slant the top stitch in either direction as long as you are consistent.

When working on double mesh you cross the stitches individually as you travel across horizontal rows alternating direction of travel (136), or work the first half and cross it with a return journey (137).

When working on single mesh over a single row of canvas thread, you must cross each stitch individually to produce even stitches. Use small Cross Stitch to achieve a beautiful, textured ground that resembles a beaded fabric (138). Use Cross Stitch over 2 by 2 canvas threads on single mesh crossed individually or crossed in 2 journeys (139). Cross the stitches individually to provide long-wearing fabric for a rug or upholstery.

Cross Stitch is one of the easiest stitches since it is not necessary to turn the work or work in diagonal rows. Because there is an equal pull in both directions, the canvas never becomes distorted.

135. Cross Stitch is a unit of 2 Half Cross Stitches.

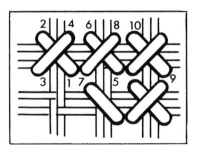

136. Cross Stitch crossed individually, on double mesh.

137. Cross Stitch crossed by a return journey, on double mesh.

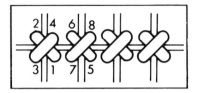

138. Cross Stitch crossed individually, on single mesh.

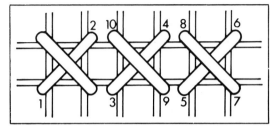

139. Cross Stitch crossed by a return journey, on single mesh, over 2 by 2 canvas threads.

Upright Cross Stitch

Also called Straight Cross Stitch

Upright Cross Stitch is a unit of 2 Straight Gobelin crossing each other perpendicularly. Cross them with either stitch on top according to a consistent plan.

When working a horizontal row with a horizontal stitch on top, skip a space between each vertical stitch. This space will be occupied by a vertical stitch in the next row (140). Travel in horizontal, vertical, or diagonal rows (141). You can also alternate the crossing (142).

This is a handsome background stitch. It may seem tedious in large areas, but it is well worth trying for its unusual pineapplelike texture. Use it to simulate pebbles, sand, and shrubbery. (See Upright Cross in section D3 of Fan Sampler.)

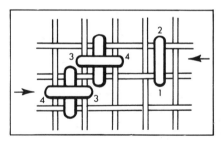

140. When traveling in horizontal rows, work one row from right to left, crossing stitches left to right. Alternate with another row traveling from left to right, crossing from right to left.

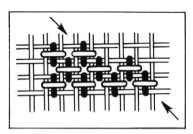

141. When traveling in diagonal rows that slant from upper left to lower right, cross the stitches from the left. Reverse procedure for rows slanting in opposite direction.

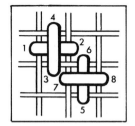

142. Cross one stitch with vertical on top, another with horizontal on top.

St. George and St. Andrew Cross Stitch

St. George and St. Andrew is a stitch pattern combining Upright Cross (St. George 143) and Cross (St. Andrew 144). Work St. George and St. Andrew in diagonal rows. It will show to the best advantage worked in 2 colors (145). Work all one color first, then fill the remaining spaces with the other color. (See the Cross Stitch swatch in color in Patchwork Sampler I.)

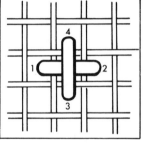

143. St. George is Upright Cross Stitch.

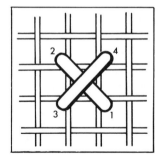

144. St. Andrew is (diagonal) Cross Stitch.

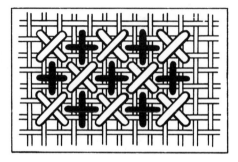

145. Enter all Cross Stitches first, in diagonal or horizontal rows, in one color. Enter Upright Cross Stitches next in diagonal rows in second color.

Canvas Lace

Canvas Lace is a Victorian fantasy; a beautiful imitation of black lace is executed in Cross Stitch using two weights of thread. The canvas itself plays an important part in the total effect. Use a fine silk thread or cotton floss for the Cross Stitch of the net ground, and a heavier-weight wool or cotton floss for the Cross Stitch pattern.

Use single mesh with Cross Stitch worked over 2 by 2 canvas threads (146). You can also work Cross Stitch over a single intersection, on a single mesh, if you cross the stitches individually. If you use interlock canvas you can use any of the methods described under Cross Stitch. Remember to cross all stitches in the same order. Use compensating Half Cross when working a net ground around Tent Stitch as in the swatch shown here. (See Canvas Lace in section E5 of Fan Sampler.)

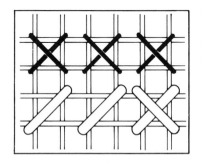

146. Work Cross Stitch over 2 by 2 on single mesh. Use very fine thread for net ground, heavy thread for pattern.

Canvas Lace border copied from Victorian sampler, bequest of Gertrude Oppenheimer to Cooper-Hewitt Museum, 1981-28-299. Using black silk sewing thread and 1-ply Nantucket Twist. On ecru 24-mesh.

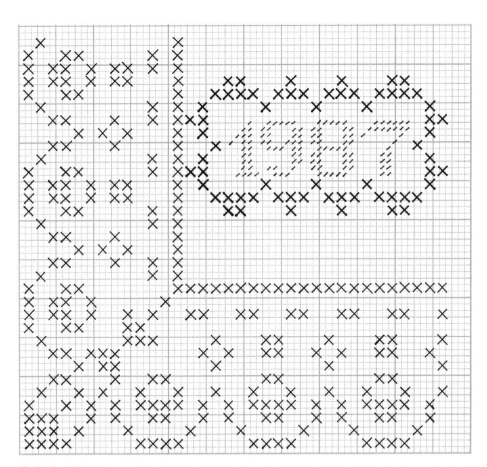

Only the Cross Stitch pattern to be worked in heavy thread is indicated. Work the remaining background in Cross Stitch over 2 by 2 canvas threads with fine silk or floss. The date is shown in Tent Stitch.

107

Woven Band

Woven Band consists of 2 opposing journeys of Slanting Gobelin creating a latticework. Use contrasting threads to dramatize the woven effect.

    Work the first journey with stitches slanting over 3, 4, or 5 intersections, skipping a space between each stitch. In a return journey, weave a second set through the first set with stitches heading in the opposite direction. Stitches in the second set emerge at the base, one mesh opening to the left of the first set (147).

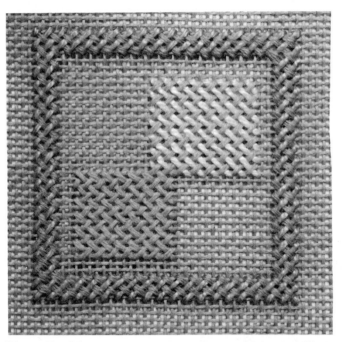

Woven Band frames a square shape. Diagonal Weaving fills 2 squares inside frame. Using 3-ply Nantucket Twist and size 3 pearl cotton. On tan 13-mesh.

Woven Band is worked over 4 intersections. Note long compensating stitches in upper right and lower left corners. Diagonal Weaving in upper square worked in 2 colors, lower square in 1 color.

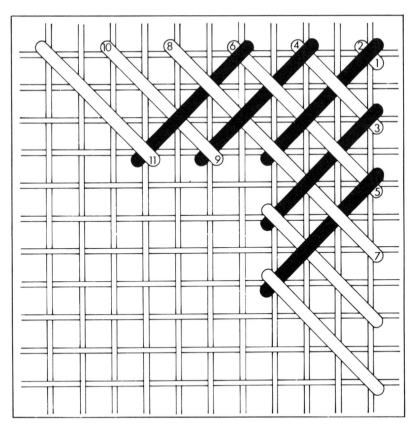

147. Start in upper right corner with Tent Stitch, then work Slanting Gobelin. Work return journey from left to right, weaving through first journey. Note compensating stitches in upper right corner. Note all 4 corners in graph for swatch.

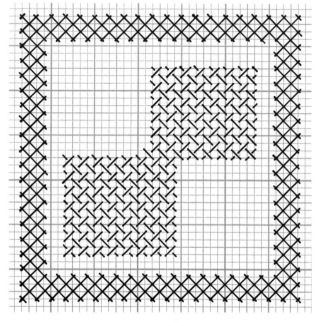

Diagonal Weaving

Diagonal Weaving is not a Cross Stitch nor is it woven, but when it is worked it appears to be crossed and it resembles the preceding Woven Band. Diagonal Weaving is the reverse side of Brick Stitch. Use 2 needles, one for each color, when alternating the colors of the rows.

Work Slanting Gobelin over 2 by 2 canvas threads, skipping a space between stitches. Drop one canvas thread for each new row, slant the stitches in the opposite direction, and enter the mesh opening crossed by the stitches in the row above. Note compensating Tent Stitch (148).

Large Cross using 4-ply Persian and Upright Cross using 3-ply Persian. On 12-mesh.

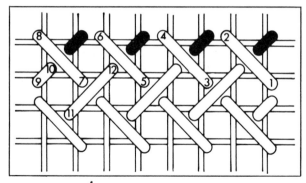

148. Start with second row; work right to left. Cross over 2, pass down under 2 across the row. Work third row left to right. Slant stitches in opposite direction. Start 1 canvas thread below row above. Cross over 2 into mesh opening crossed by row above. Work compensating stitches last in first row. Remember that this is back side of Brick Stitch. All stitches are slanted and pass under 2, producing straight stitches on the back of the work.

Large and Upright Cross Stitch

Large Cross Stitch and Upright Cross Stitch are combined to create a pattern. Work the Large Cross first over 4 by 4 canvas threads, crossing each stitch individually. Travel in horizontal rows that alternate direction. After completing all rows of Large Cross, place an Upright Cross over 2 by 2 canvas threads in the open space between each Large Cross Stitch (149). This stitch is particularly attractive worked in contrasting colors and textures.

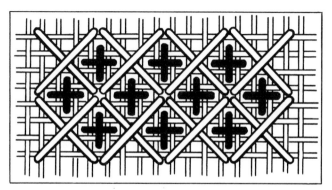

149. Work Large Cross first, then fill open spaces with Upright Cross.

109

Oblong Cross Stitch

Oblong Cross Stitch is a Cross Stitch taken over 2 vertical canvas threads by 3, 4, or 5 horizontal canvas threads (150). You can arrange Oblong Cross on the canvas in an infinite number of variations, combining it with many other stitches. Try filling the space left open between the Long Cross in a contrasting color or texture with smaller Cross Stitch (151, 152, 153) or with Straight Gobelin Stitch (154).

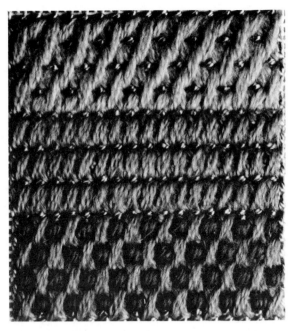

Band 1: Worked as diagram 153. Band 2: Worked as diagram 154. Band 3: Worked as diagram 151. Using 3-ply Persian and size 3 pearl cotton. On 12-mesh.

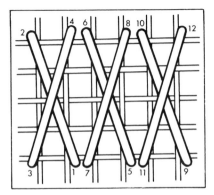

150. Oblong Cross over 5 horizontal canvas threads.

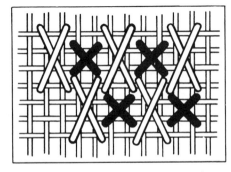

151. A first row of Oblong Cross taken over 4 horizontal canvas threads skipping 2 vertical threads between each stitch. A second row encroaches 1 canvas thread into the row above. The third row is the same as the first, the fourth is the same as the second. Cross Stitch fills the open space.

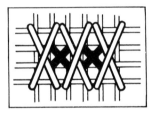

152. Oblong Cross over 4 canvas threads. Cross Stitch over 2 fills the open space.

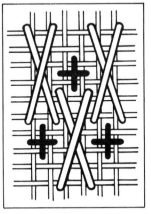

153. Oblong Cross over 6, encroaching by 2. Upright Cross fills the open space.

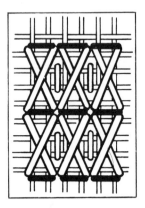

154. Rows of Oblong Cross over 4 with Straight Gobelin in between; Back Stitch over 2 between the rows.

Crossed Corners Stitch

Also called Rice Stitch

Crossed Corners Stitch is a unit composed of a large Cross Stitch crossed at the end of each arm.

Work a large Cross Stitch over 4 by 4 canvas threads (155). Cross opposite corners over 2 by 2 canvas threads, crossing one arm, then the other (156 and 157). Use finer and shinier thread for the corner stitches for a more striking effect.

When working a large area of Crossed Corners, it is easier to work all Cross Stitch first in alternating horizontal rows. Then cross the corners traveling in diagonal rows, as though working long Diagonal Tent Stitch.

To cover grin-through around the square units and to sharply define them, you can work Back Stitch over 2 canvas threads using a single ply of fine matching thread (158). (See Crossed Corners in section H4 of Fan Sampler.)

Crossed Corners, using 4-ply Nantucket Twist for large Cross Stitch and size 3 pearl cotton for corners. On 12-mesh. Use this stitch for a handsome textured picture frame.

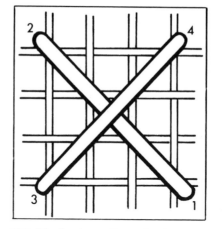

155. Work a large Cross Stitch.

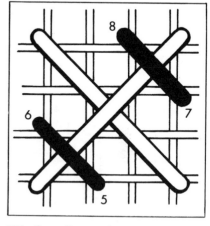

156. Cross 2 opposite corners.

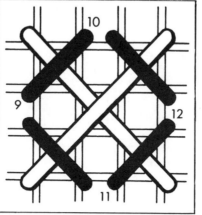

157. Cross the other 2 corners.

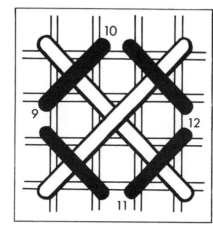

158. Four Crossed Corner Stitches with Back Stitch.

Double Cross Stitch

Double Cross Stitch is a composite of Upright Cross and Cross Stitch. Work an Upright Cross over 4 by 4 canvas threads (159). Cross Stitch over it covering 2 by 2 canvas threads (160). Work the large Upright Cross first traveling in diagonal rows, then work the Cross Stitch in horizontal rows in a contrasting thread (161). You can easily leave diamond-shaped spaces between some of the units to fill with Diamond Eyelet (162).

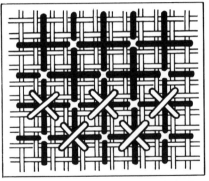

161. When using contrasting threads, work Upright Cross in diagonal rows, then Double Cross them in horizontal rows.

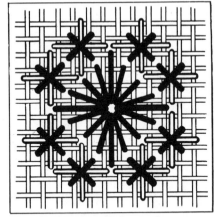

162. Omit some stitches to leave space for ornamental ones, such as Diamond Eyelet worked over 8 canvas threads in each direction.

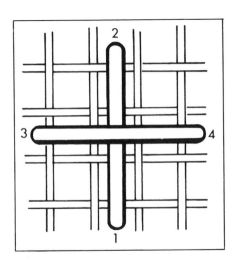

159. Work a large Upright Cross Stitch.

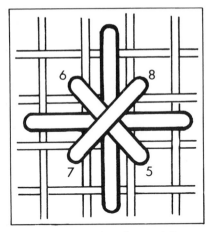

160. Cross it with a diagonal Cross Stitch. When using one thread, cross each unit individually.

Upright Cross, using 2-ply Persian, Cross Stitch over it and Diamond Eyelet, using size 3 pearl cotton. Diamond Eyelet occupies space of 4 Double Cross Stitch. On 12-mesh.

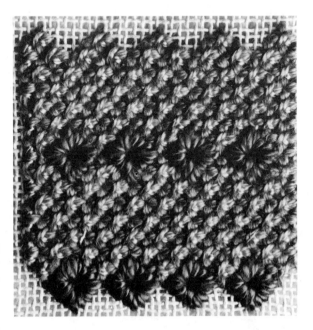

Smyrna Stitch

Smyrna is a composite of Cross and Upright Cross Stitch. Work a Cross Stitch first over 4 by 4 or 2 by 2 canvas threads (163). Work an Upright Cross over it occupying the same number of canvas threads (164 and 165). Cross the Cross Stitch once as a Smyrna variation (166). See this variation in Flower Picture II, where it is used on the basket. If you require a fuller stitch, try Leviathan (170 to 173), which occupies all the mesh openings around a square of 4 by 4 canvas threads.

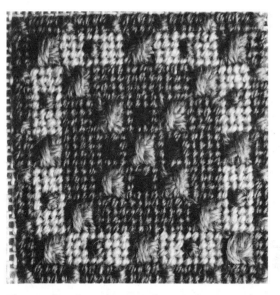

The smaller decorative stitches are Smyrna taken over 2 canvas threads. The larger decorative stitches are Leviathan. The background is Tent Stitch. All stitches are worked in 2-ply Persian on 12-mesh.

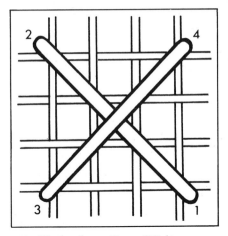

163. Work a large Cross Stitch over 4 by 4 canvas threads.

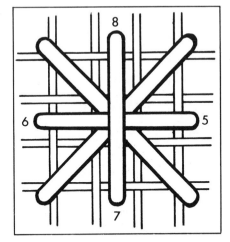

164. Work an Upright Cross Stitch on top of it. Note that some canvas threads are exposed at the perimeter.

165. Smyrna worked over 2 by 2 canvas threads. Note that all canvas threads are covered at the perimeter.

166. Smyrna crossed once.

Triple Cross Stitch

Triple Cross Stitch is a composite of 2 Oblong Cross Stitch and a large Cross Stitch. Work a horizontal Oblong Cross over 1 horizontal by 3 vertical canvas threads (167). Cross this with a vertical Oblong Cross over 3 horizontal by 1 vertical canvas thread (168). Finally, cross the entire unit with a diagonal Cross Stitch taken over 3 by 3 canvas threads (169). Because Triple Cross Stitch occupies an uneven number of canvas threads and most needlepoint stitches occupy an even number, you will find Triple Cross a very useful stitch to have in your needlepoint vocabulary.

Medium-size stitches are Triple Cross, small stitches are Smyrna, 4 large stitches are Leviathan, background is Diagonal Tent. Using 2-ply Persian. On 12-mesh.

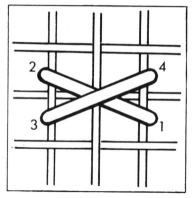

167. Work the first Oblong Cross on its side.

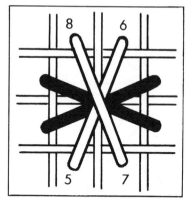

168. Work the second Oblong Cross standing up.

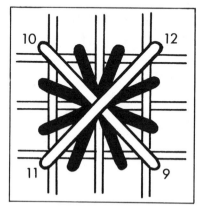

169. Work a large diagonal Cross Stitch over all.

Leviathan Stitch

Leviathan Stitch is composed of a large Cross Stitch with both of its arms crossed diagonally and an Upright Cross worked over the entire unit.

Work Cross Stitch over 4 by 4 canvas threads (170). Next, cross the first arm twice (171). Then cross the other arm twice (172). Work an Upright Cross over all the Cross Stitches (173).

I prefer using Leviathan as a raised stitch when filling an area of 4 by 4 canvas threads to Smyrna because it covers the canvas threads so neatly. See the preceding stitch swatch for examples of Leviathan.

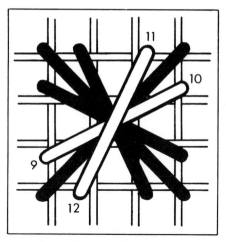

172. Cross the second arm diagonally following the numbers.

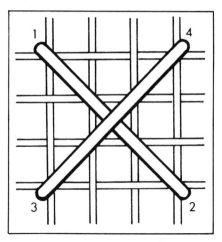

170. First work a large Cross Stitch over 4 by 4 canvas threads. Note that the first arm emerges at the upper left.

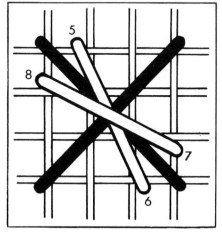

171. Cross the first arm diagonally following the numbers.

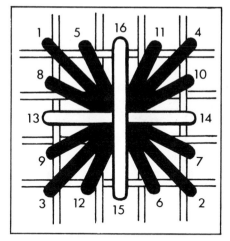

173. Complete Leviathan with an Upright Cross on top.

Herringbone Stitch, Herringbone-Gone-Wrong

Herringbone Stitch is composed of opposing Slanting Gobelin that cross top and bottom as they travel across horizontal rows.

Work Slanting Gobelin from upper left to lower right across 4 intersections. Pass under 2 canvas threads to the left. Work another Slanting Gobelin from lower left to upper right and pass under 2 canvas threads to the left. Repeat these movements across the row. Note compensating stitches at either end (174). Drop down 2 canvas threads to work the next row. Work all rows starting from the left for the same overlapping, or start from the opposite side and pass under each previous stitch (175). A handsome variation is Herringbone-Gone-Wrong; start each row at opposite sides (176). (See Herringbone-Gone-Wrong in section E2 of Fan Sampler.)

Herringbone Bands and fillings using 4-ply Nantucket Twist and Cairo matte cotton. On 13-mesh.

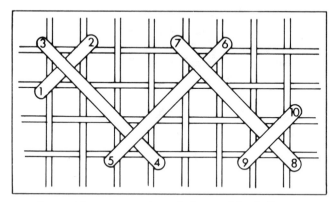

174. Start with compensating stitch over 2 by 2. Pass under 2 to left, long stitch down, pass under 2 to left, long stitch up, etc.

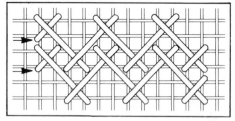

175. Same as 174 for first row. Drop down 2 canvas threads and repeat first row for each new row. To alternate direction of row and achieve same overlapping, pass under each previous stitch with each new one.

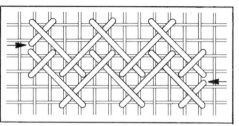

176. Alternate direction of row to produce Herringbone-Gone-Wrong.

Herringbone Border

Herringbone Border is a single band of Herringbone Stitch worked in many journeys across a row from left to right, occupying the same horizontal canvas threads, but interlacing subsequent vertical canvas threads. You can work over 4 to 8 horizontal canvas threads with up to 6 journeys. For a striking border, use close values plus 1 accent color.

Start with a first journey over 6 canvas threads. Occupy the next pair of vertical canvas threads along the bottom and top edges of the band with each new journey. Note the compensating stitches at both ends of the border (177). (See Herringbone Border in section F3 of Fan Sampler.)

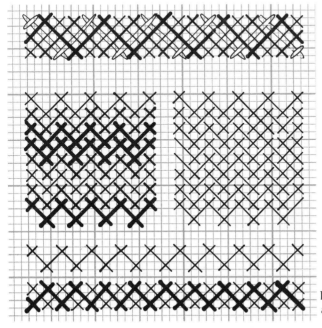

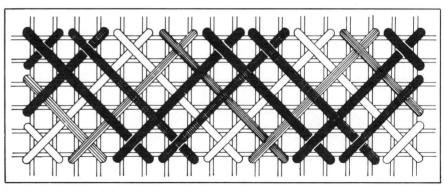

177. Use up to 6 different working threads in overlapping journeys for a Herringbone Border.

Band at top is over 6 canvas threads, all other Herringbone is over 4.

Squared Herringbone Stitch

Squared Herringbone Stitch has unusual depth; Herringbone Stitch worked in a diamond shape travels around a center Cross Stitch building up a series of overlapping stitches. The stitches lengthen with each journey and the center seems deeper inside. Travel in 1, 2, 3, or 4 journeys but close each unit neatly with the last stitch passing under the first leg of the trip around (178). You need an even number of canvas threads for this stitch and a fine working thread.

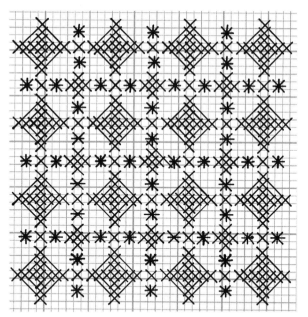

Squared Herringbone combines well with other stitches as shown here. Connect Squared Herringbone Stitches with Cross Stitch in horizontal and vertical rows. Then create a plaid by working small Squared Herringbone alternating with Smyrna Stitch in horizontal and vertical rows that cross the Cross Stitch.

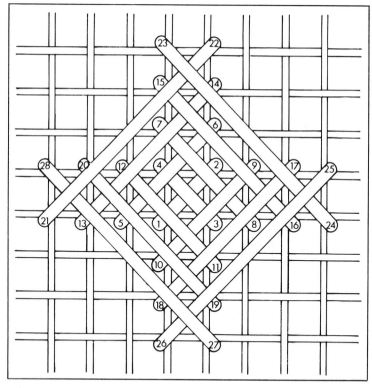

178. Start with a Cross Stitch. Herringbone Stitch around it. Come out at odd numbers and enter even ones. Complete each unit by passing the last stitch under and into the back, as with 27 under 21.

Squared Herringbone plaid using size 5 pearl cotton. On 12-mesh.

118

Waffle Stitch

Waffle Stitch is a square unit that starts with a Cross Stitch over which Herringbone Stitch revolves to produce great depth.

Start with Cross Stitch over a square of 5, 7, 9, 11, 13, or 15. Follow the number sequence in diagram 179; travel clockwise around the perimeter and occupy all mesh openings. Complete each unit, passing the last slanting stitch under the first one of that revolution, as with 19 passing under 13 (179).

Change color to create patterns (180 and 181). Use fine thread, light values, and an odd number of canvas threads. Cross corners to create variations (182 and 183).

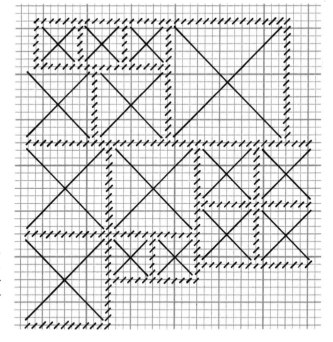

Waffle worked over 5, 7, 9, and 15 intersections. Cross Stitch over 1 intersection separates all Waffle units.

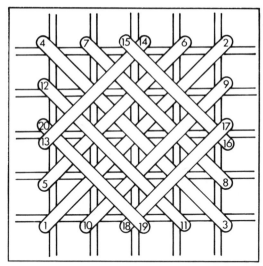

179. Cross Stitch over 5 by 5 intersections. Follow numbers, crossing and recrossing in an orderly pattern. Emerge at odd number, enter an even one.

Waffle Stitch using 1-ply Medicis and 3-ply Nantucket Twist. Cross Stitch using size 5 pearl cotton. On 13-mesh.

(continued)

(Waffle Stitch, *continued*)

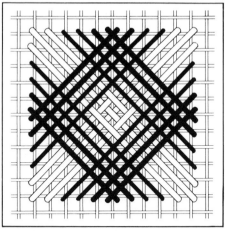

180. Cross Stitch over 11 by 11 intersections. Change color after 3 long crosses appear, shown in white.

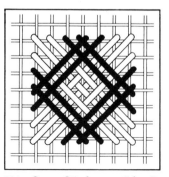

181. Cross Stitch over 7 by 7 intersections. Change color after 3 long crosses appear, shown in white.

182. Cross Stitch over 11 by 11 intersections. Complete all crossings. Cross all corners 5 times with another color, shown in black.

183. Cross Stitch over 7 by 7 intersections. Change color for last journey. Cross each corner twice, shown in black.

Rhodes Stitch

Rhodes Stitch is a unit of long overlapping stitches that revolve around a square, creating a pyramid. Start a unit with a long diagonal stitch across a square; the square can have either an even or odd number of intersections. Proceed counterclockwise, emerging at the base to the right of the previous stitch and entering at the top to the left of the previous one. There will be a handsome pile-up of thread in the center of the square (184).

Use fine smooth thread; light values show up best. You can work parts of a stitch as a variation (see this on the swatch), change color in the middle of a unit (185), tie a unit down in the center (186), or cross the corners if you use an even number of canvas threads (187).

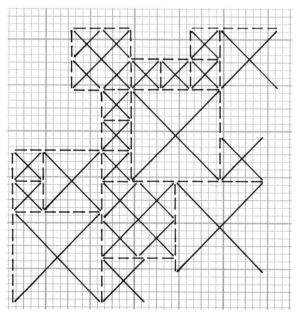

Rhodes Stitch units vary in size; 4-, 6-, 8-, 10-, and 12-mesh square. Work Back Stitch over 2 canvas threads between all stitches.

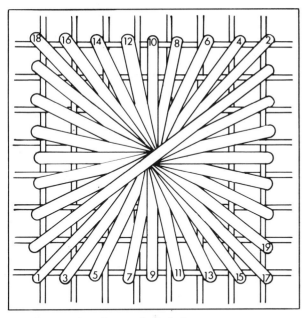

184. Start with a diagonal stitch from corner to corner. Then follow the number sequence, moving counterclockwise, using all mesh openings of the perimeter.

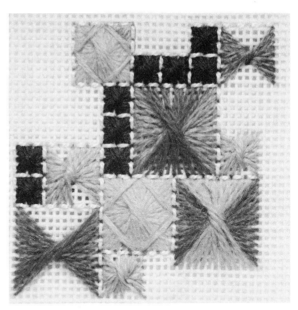

Rhodes Stitch using 1-ply Persian, 2-ply Nantucket Twist, 1-ply Medicis. Back Stitch using size 5 pearl cotton. On 13-mesh.

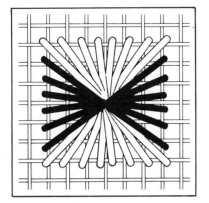

185. Work half the stitch in one color, other half in another. Or work just half a stitch.

186. Tie Rhodes Stitch down in the center.

187. Cross the corners with another color.

121

Long-armed Cross Stitch

Also called Long-legged Cross Stitch and Portuguese Stitch

Long-armed Cross is the first Cross Stitch of a series that moves ahead with a long arm and back with a shorter one, traveling back and forth across the canvas. Start with a Cross Stitch; the first arm heads in the direction of the row. Thus, if you are working left to right, the first half of the Cross Stitch slants from lower left to upper right (188). The next stitch is a long arm. Come out the same opening as the first stitch and cross over 4 vertical canvas threads. Pass the needle down under 2 (189). Cross back over 2 and go down under 2 (190). Repeat the process, starting with the long arm (191).

This may seem complicated at first, but it is really quite easy and suitable for beginners. The second row travels in the opposite direction, from right to left. Start with a Cross Stitch; this time slant the first arm from lower right to upper left (192). Note the compensating stitches that close both of these rows (191 and 192).

Beautiful needlepoint rugs from Portugal are worked with this stitch. It is very long-wearing, useful for church kneelers as well for this reason. You can work small Long-armed Cross Stitch on double mesh by treating each set of double threads as 2 single mesh. Because this stitch is always worked over 2 mesh, there is no need to prick apart the vertical canvas threads.

Long-armed Cross looks very much like Greek Stitch, which follows. One way to tell them apart is that Long-armed Cross makes vertical stitches on the back and Greek Stitch makes horizontal ones.

188. Start with a Cross Stitch over 2 by 2 canvas threads.

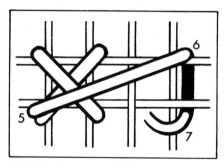

189. Work a long stitch across 4 vertical canvas threads.

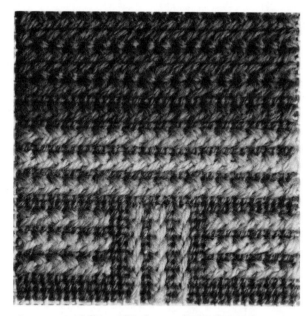

Long-armed Cross Stitch travels in alternating rows at top of swatch. Remaining rows alternate Long-armed Cross worked left to right with Tent worked right to left. Using 2-ply Persian. On 12-mesh.

190. Cross back over 2 vertical canvas threads.

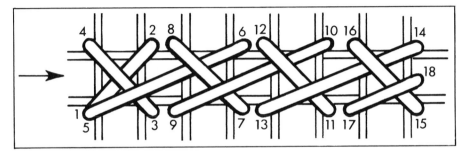

191. Complete the row working from left to right. Note the row ends with a compensating stitch that covers a canvas thread that would otherwise be covered with a long arm.

Long-armed Cross is an excellent stitch for needlepoint rugs. Using 2 full strands Persian or rug wool works very rapidly. Consider double threads on double mesh as 2 canvas threads. On 3½ double mesh.

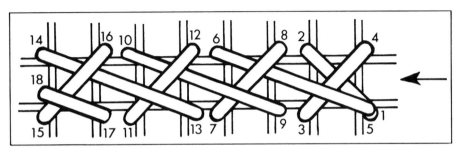

192. Complete a row worked right to left. A similar compensating stitch is taken at the far end.

Greek Stitch

Greek Stitch, like Long-armed Cross, travels ahead with a long cross and back with a shorter one. Greek Stitch starts with a Cross Stitch that emerges at the top.

Start with a Cross Stitch over 2 by 2 canvas threads (193). Emerge once more at the top of the cross; work a long arm down across 4 vertical canvas threads and back under 2 (194). Emerge and cross over 2 vertical canvas threads (195). Repeat the process, starting again with the long arm; end each row with a compensating stitch (196).

Greek Stitch is worked from left to right. Turn the canvas upside down at the end of each row to travel in the same direction. Since this is a Cross Stitch pulled evenly in both directions it need not be stretched on a frame. Start all rows with a Cross Stitch and close with a compensating stitch.

Greek Stitch with a pattern of color changes. Close the row as in 196 with each color change, or flow colors together by working part of stitch in one color and part in another. Using 2-ply Persian. On 12-mesh.

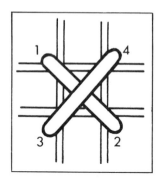

193. Work a Cross Stitch emerging at upper left.

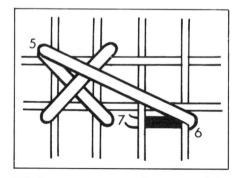

194. Emerge once more from upper left and cross over 4 canvas threads.

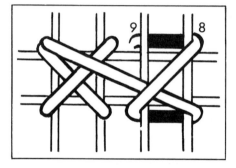

195. Pass under 2 canvas threads to the left and cross over 2 to the right.

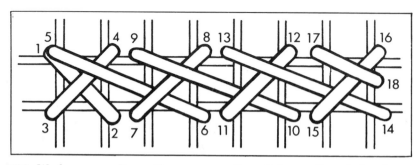

196. Work a row ending with a compensating stitch over 2 vertical and 1 horizontal canvas threads.

Plait Stitch

Plait Stitch is similar to Long-armed Cross; it travels ahead with a long diagonal arm and crosses back with a shorter one. Plait Stitch travels slowly, advancing 2 and back 1.

Emerge at lower left; work on Oblong Cross. Emerge again at lower right and cross back 1 vertical canvas thread (197). Emerge directly below and cross ahead 2 canvas threads (198). Continue to move forward 2 and back 1 (199). Work Plait Stitch over any number of canvas threads (200). Use it over folded edges of interlock canvas to bind edges of accessories.

Gobelin Plait Stitch

Gobelin Plait Stitch gives a woven look by alternating rows of slanting stitches that cross each other at the base.

Work a row of Slanting Gobelin over 2 by 2 canvas threads from left to right. Drop down 1 canvas thread for the second row and work right to left, with stitches slanting in the opposite direction. Work each stitch directly under the one in the row above, crossing it at its base, entering the opening between the stitches. Work every other row alike (201). Note that Gobelin Plait resembles Diagonal Weaving (148) but is more dense.

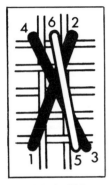 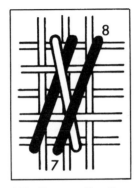 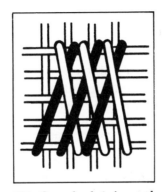

197. Work Oblong Cross, emerge at lower right, cross back 1.

198. Emerge directly under point of entry and cross forward 2.

199. Cross back 1, forward 2, back 1, forward 2.

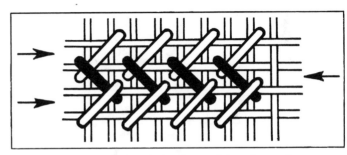

201. Row 1: Travel left to right, forward 2 and over 2. Row 2: Drop 1, travel right to left, forward 2 and over 2 into row 1. Alternate rows.

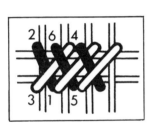

200. Plait Stitch can be worked over 2, 3, 4, or 5 canvas threads.

Gobelin Plait, at top, in rows of different colors. Frame with mitered corners in Plait Stitch over 5 canvas threads. Plait Stitch edging over 2 canvas threads, using 3-ply Persian. On 12-mesh.

Tied, Looped, and Raised Stitches

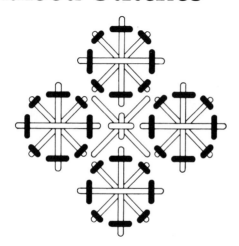

Shell Stitch

Also called Sheaf Stitch and Wheat Stitch

Shell Stitch is composed of 4 Straight Gobelin, taken over 4, 5, or 6 horizontal canvas threads, and tied down in the center with a horizontal stitch (202). Work 4 Straight Gobelin over 6 canvas threads, come out to the left of the center vertical canvas thread, encircle the 4 straight stitches, and enter the mesh opening to the right of the center canvas thread (203). Fill the space between stitch units with Upright Cross Stitch; cover the exposed canvas between the rows with Back Stitch (204). Work a coil between the first and second sheaf, then between the second and third, linking all "sheaves" together (205). (See this stitch in section H1 of Fan Sampler.)

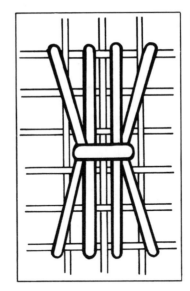

202. Single Shell Stitch over 6 canvas threads.

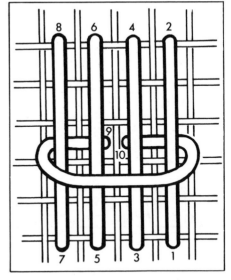

203. Note the points of exit and entry on either side of the center vertical canvas thread.

Shell Stitch using 2-ply Persian. Both Back Stitch and coils use size 5 pearl cotton. Upright Cross, using 7-ply French silk. On 10-mesh.

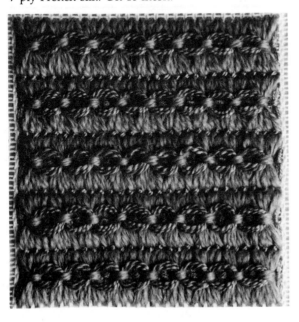

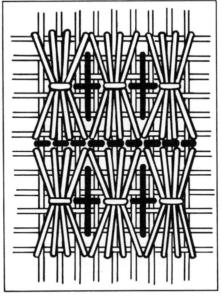

204. Work Upright Cross between sheaves and Back Stitch between rows to cover exposed canvas threads.

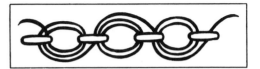

205. Work coil from right to left. Pass around first 2 tie-downs 3 times clockwise, then pass around second and third tie-downs 3 times counterclockwise. Continue alternating the coiling.

Tied Oblong Cross Stitch

Oblong Cross Stitch is an Oblong Cross tied down with Back Stitch. First work the Oblong Cross over 4 or 6 canvas threads. Then, with contrasting color, work Back Stitch over 2 canvas threads across the middle of the cross (206). Tied Oblong Cross is particularly striking when taken over 6 horizontal canvas threads and tied down with 3 rows of Back Stitch in 2 or 3 colors (207).

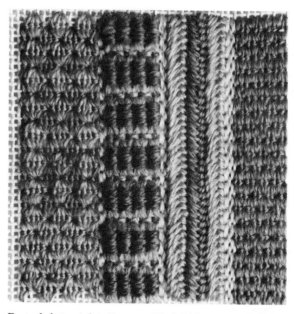

From left to right: Rococo, Tied Oblong Cross, Fishbone, French, with staggered Back Stitch between the columns. Rococo, using 1-ply Persian; Tied Oblong Cross over 6 canvas threads, tied 3 times, using 2-ply Persian; Fishbone, using 2-ply Persian; and French Stitch, using 1-ply Persian. Back Stitch between columns over 2 canvas threads, using 1-ply Persian. On 14-mesh.

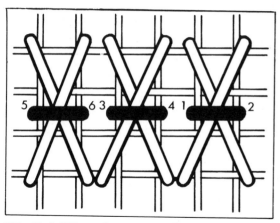

206. Tied Oblong Cross over 4 horizontal canvas threads, tied down once at the cross.

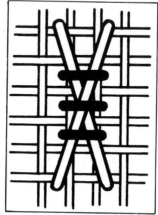

207. Tied Oblong Cross over 6 horizontal canvas threads, tied down 3 times.

Tied Double Cross Stitch

Also called Asterisk Stitch

Tied Double Cross Stitch is a variation of Double Cross Stitch that employs Back Stitch to tie down the spokes. First work a Diagonal Cross over 4 by 4 canvas threads. On top of this work an Upright Cross over 6 by 6 canvas threads. Work Back Stitch over the end of each spoke, passing over 2 canvas threads to tie down the Upright Cross and over 1 intersection to tie down the Cross Stitch (208).

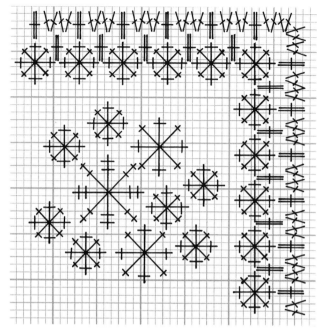

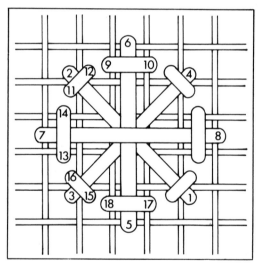

208. Back Stitch around the spokes of a Double Cross Stitch.

The outer border is worked with Knotted Stitch slanting in alternate directions, alternating with Double and Tie Stitch. Inside border is worked with small Tied Double Cross Stitch alternating with Double and Tie, and French Knot. Inside the square, Tied Double Cross is worked over 10, 8, 6, and 4 canvas threads.

Tied Double Cross Stitch, using sizes 3 and 5 pearl cotton. Double and Tie, Knotted Stitch, using Swedish linen. On linen canvas, 13-mesh.

Double and Tie Stitch

Double and Tie Stitch is a unit of 2 Straight Gobelin taken between 2 canvas threads and tied down in the middle over 2 canvas threads. Work 2 Straight Gobelin over 4 canvas threads, sharing the space between 2 vertical canvas threads (209). Tie them down over 2 vertical canvas threads, coming out on one side and going in on the other (210). Work Double and Tie Stitch in diagonal rows (211). Use it for a long-wearing rug. (See Double and Tie in section D4 of Fan Sampler.)

Double and Tie worked in diagonal rows, each row a different color. Using rug wool or 2 full strands Persian, work a bold contemporary rug quickly with this stitch. Alternate the slant of the diagonal rows for a stunning zigzag pattern.

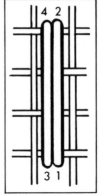

209. Two Straight Gobelin Stitches are taken in one location.

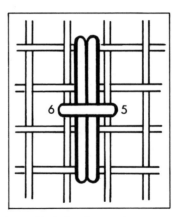

210. Back Stitch ties the 2 stitches down.

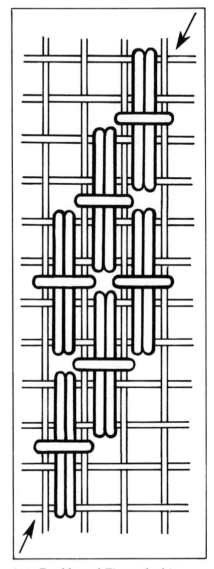

211. Double and Tie worked in diagonal rows. Complete each unit before going on to next stitch.

130

Knotted Stitch

Knotted Stitch is an oblique stitch tied down in the middle with a reversed Tent Stitch. Take a slanted stitch over 3 horizontal and 1 vertical canvas threads. Tie it down over the center intersection, coming out the upper left and going in the lower right (212). In the first row, travel right to left and tie down in this manner. In the second row, travel left to right and tie down from lower right to upper left (213). Alternate these two rows. As a variation, you can alternate the oblique slant of the Knotted Stitch. (See an example of this variation on the Tied Double Cross Stitch swatch. Note that much of the canvas is left open.)

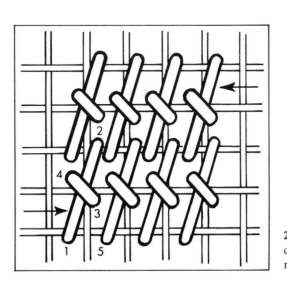

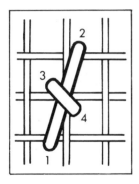

212. Tie each stitch down individually, away from the direction in which the row is traveling.

Knotted Stitch, using 2-ply Persian. Pattern is created purely with use of color. On 12-mesh.

213. Work rows in alternate directions. Note how the second row encroaches on the first.

131

Fishbone Stitch

Fishbone Stitch is a Slanting Gobelin tied down at one end. The Gobelin can slant in either direction and can be tied down at either end.

To work a Fishbone pointing up, slant a Gobelin over 3 by 3 canvas threads; emerge lower left and go in upper right. Emerge 1 space below point of entry and go in at upper left, making a reverse Tent Stitch at the top (214).

To work a Fishbone pointing down, reverse the procedure. Emerge upper left and go in lower right. Emerge 1 space to left of point of entry and go in upper right, making a Tent Stitch at the base (215).

Work a vertical row, dropping a canvas thread for each stitch, taking identical stitches one under the other. Point the Fishbone in each row in the opposite direction (216).

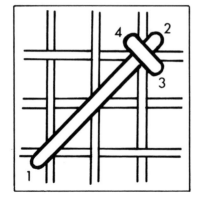

214. Fishbone Stitch tied at the top with a reverse Tent Stitch.

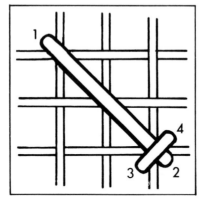

215. Fishbone Stitch slanting in the opposite direction and tied at the base with a Tent Stitch.

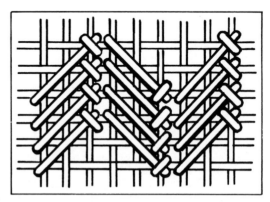

216. Fishbone Stitch worked in vertical rows, each row slanting in an alternate direction.

Web Stitch

Web Stitch is composed of a series of diagonal stitches tied down at regular intervals over intersections of canvas threads. Start in a corner position with a Tent Stitch. Take lengths of graduated slanting stitches, tying each one down as you progress. The slanting stitches grow 1 canvas thread longer as they move to the next mesh opening at the side and top (217). Tie down either every other canvas thread (218) or every canvas thread (219). Web Stitch looks best worked in cotton or silk floss. (See Web Stitch in section G4 of Fan Sampler.)

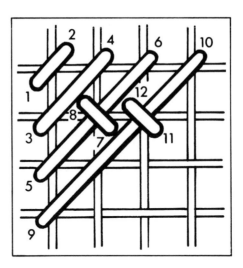

217. Each slanting stitch, beginning with the third, is tied down as it is made. Note that in this diagram no tie-downs are worked at the edges, although it is possible to do so.

Checkerboard design created by working Web Stitch in even squares. Every other square worked with the top of the canvas held at the side to change direction. Using 7-ply French silk. On 12-mesh.

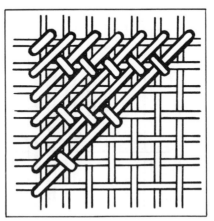

218. Web Stitch with tie-downs over every other horizontal canvas thread.

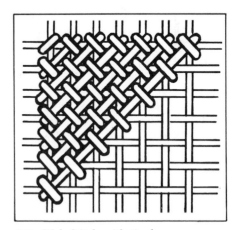

219. Web Stitch with tie-downs over every canvas thread.

French Stitch

French Stitch is a unit of 2 Straight Gobelin taken between 2 canvas threads, each tied down individually. Work 1 Straight Gobelin over 4 horizontal canvas threads; tie it down from left to right (220). Work a second Straight Gobelin, sharing the same space; tie it down from right to left (221). Note that both tying stitches are taken from the outside of the stitch into the center. Work stitches in diagonal rows (222). French Stitch provides a nice rough texture. (See it worked in the Tied Oblong Cross Stitch swatch.)

Rococo Stitch worked in diagonal rows to make diamond and zigzag design. Note that the pattern is achieved strictly by use of color. Using 2-ply Persian. On 12-mesh. (See Rococo Stripes worked in horizontal rows in the Tied Oblong Stitch swatch.)

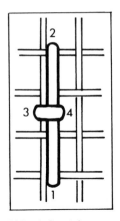

220. A Straight Gobelin is tied to the vertical canvas thread on the left.

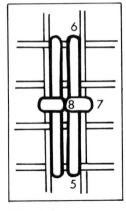

221. A second Gobelin in the same space is tied to the vertical canvas thread on the right.

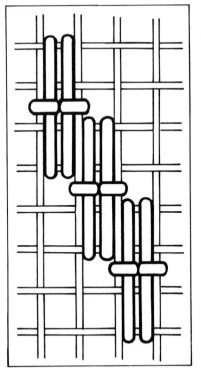

222. French Stitch is worked in diagonal rows. Complete each unit before going on to the next.

Rococo Stitch

Rococo Stitch is a unit of 4 Straight Gobelin taken over 4 horizontal canvas threads, sharing the same top and bottom mesh openings; each is tied down to a different vertical canvas thread. One at a time, work each stitch of the unit. Come out at the base, go in at the top, and tie it down from left to right (223–226). Work this stitch in horizontal, vertical, or diagonal rows and create patterns by changing colors. Rococo is a very old, unique, lacy-looking filling stitch.

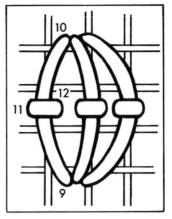

225. The third Gobelin is tied to the third vertical canvas thread.

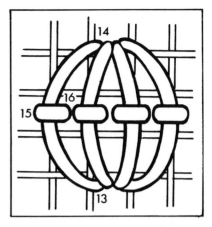

226. The fourth Gobelin is tied to the last vertical canvas thread. Note the first 2 Straight Gobelin fan to the right since they are tied to the right. The last 2 fan to the left since they are tied to the left.

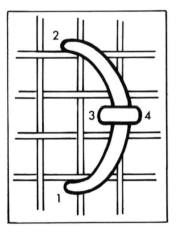

223. Each Rococo unit uses 4 horizontal by 4 vertical canvas threads. The first Straight Gobelin is made and tied to the first vertical canvas thread.

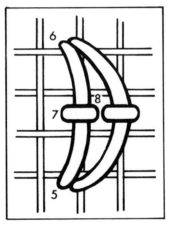

224. The second Gobelin is made and tied down to the second vertical canvas thread.

227. Four units of Rococo Stitch share the same mesh opening and create an eyelet effect.

135

Turkey Knot Stitch

Also called Turkey Work and Turkey Knot Tufting

Turkey Knot Stitch is the first of three looped stitches that create a raised pile. They can all be used to make shag rugs, fringes, and for raised effects, such as animal fur or foliage. All rows are worked horizontally from left to right. If a vertical row is needed, give the canvas a quarter turn. Progress row by row from the bottom up so that the pile does not cover the unworked area. A row or two of canvas may be left bare between rows of stitches depending on the fullness desired.

In starting a row, note that the tail end of the working thread is on the front of the canvas and that the stitch starts by going in at 1. Leave about an inch of thread on the front. Come out the next mesh opening on the left. With the thread *above* the needle, enter the mesh opening 2 canvas threads to the right, come out the original opening, and draw the thread to form a horizontal stitch (228). Use your thumb to hold the thread at the desired length of loop, enter the mesh opening 2 canvas threads to the right, and emerge one opening to the left (229). While still holding the loop with your thumb, draw up the loop, throw the working thread *above* the needle, and make another horizontal stitch by going in at 3 and coming out at 4 (230). Loops may be left uncut or clipped to the desired height or heights (231). For a deep, soft pile, use Persian, and of course it need not be separated first.

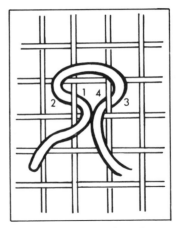

228. The tail end of working thread is on the front, the needle enters at 1, comes out to the left at 2; the thread is above the needle, enters at 3 and comes out at 4.

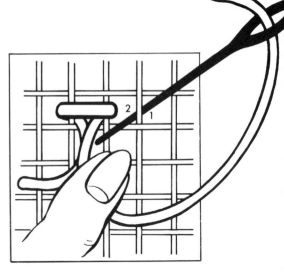

229. Use your thumb to determine the size of the loop; go in at 1 and come out at 2, forming a loop.

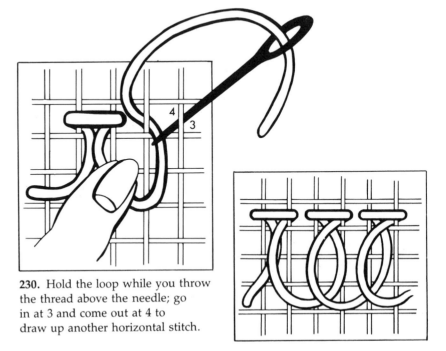

230. Hold the loop while you throw the thread above the needle; go in at 3 and come out at 4 to draw up another horizontal stitch.

231. The loops fall between the horizontal stitches.

Fringed Turkey Knot using 2-ply Persian. Fringe is shaded, each row using a different value of the same color. A single canvas thread is skipped between the rows. On 14-mesh.

Velvet Stitch

Also called Astrakhan Velvet Stitch

Velvet Stitch is another looped stitch with pile to use for rugs, fringe, or raised texture. Like Turkey Knot, work from left to right, and work up from the bottom of the canvas. If you want less bulk, leave 1 or 2 horizontal canvas threads between the rows. All looped stitches are big thread-eaters, so use long double-length thread to avoid constant starting and ending.

Work over 2 vertical by 2 horizontal canvas threads if using single mesh, over 1 or 2 sets of vertical and horizontal threads if using double mesh. Start with a Half Cross Stitch (232). Bring needle up once again from the base of the stitch. Use your thumb to hold the size loop you want, go back in at the top of the stitch, and come out directly below, under 2 canvas threads (233). Hold the loop to the left of the needle and close the stitch to make a Cross Stitch. Emerge from the next vacant lower left mesh opening to start the next stitch (234). Loops may be left uncut or trimmed to the desired height.

Two bands of Velvet Stitch. Top band shows 3 rows of cut Velvet Stitch. Lower band shows 2 rows of uncut Velvet Stitch, with a row of Tied Oblong Cross embellishing it at the top. This produces a fringe trim suitable for a pillow edging. Using 3-ply Persian. On 12-mesh.

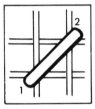

232. A Half Cross Stitch.

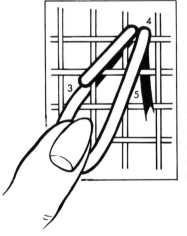

233. Come out the same opening, hold the loop, reenter the same opening, come out 2 threads below.

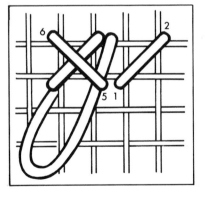

234. Hold loop to the left, work a Cross Stitch, emerge and start the next stitch at 1.

Surrey Stitch

Surrey Stitch is still another looped stitch with pile that can be used for rugs, fringe, or raised texture. As with the others, work from left to right, up from the bottom of the canvas. To work a large area, use long strands of thread to avoid too frequent starting and ending. Work Surrey over 2 vertical by 2 horizontal canvas threads. If small even loops are desired, use a knitting needle to hold the loops in place.

Start with the tail end of the thread on the front of the canvas. Go in at the top and come out 2 canvas threads directly below (235). Flip the tail end down; hold it with your thumb to the left, just below the stitch. Flip the other end of the thread above and over the work; go in 2 vertical threads to the right and come out at the top of the stitch, with the needle in front of the thread (236). Draw the needle through and the first stitch is made (237).

Hold the thread with your thumb to establish the size of the loop. Go in the third mesh opening on the top and come out 2 canvas threads below. The needle should be on top of the thumb-held loop (238). Draw the thread through, still holding the loop. Flip the working thread above and over the work, go in 2 vertical canvas threads to the right and come out drawing the thread through at the top of the loop (239). The second stitch is made. Work all other stitches in the same manner as the second stitch.

Surrey Stitch worked from the base up for 3 rows, each row in different value from dark to light. Note these loops are clipped. Note Surrey at top of swatch is left unclipped. Using 2-ply Persian. On 12-mesh.

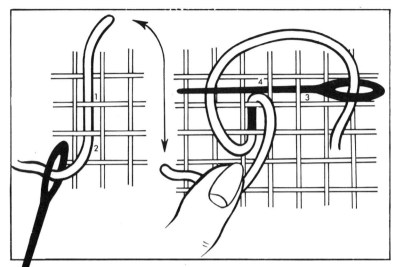 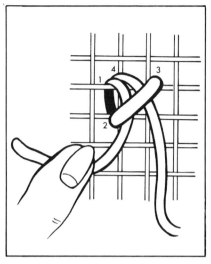

235. Tail end of thread on top, come out at base.

236. Hold tail of thread down to the left, flip thread up and over, go in 3, come out 4 in front of thread.

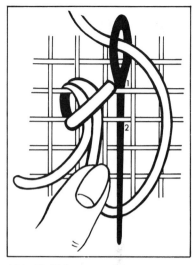

237. Draw thread through. The first stitch is made without a loop.

238. Hold loop, go in at 1, out at 2; loop falls between stitches.

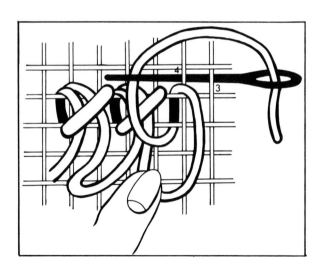

239. Hold loop, flip thread up and over, go in at 3, out at 4, in front of the thread. Draw thread through.

Buttonhole Stitch

Also called Blanket Stitch

Buttonhole Stitch is familiar to most people from experience with hand sewing. This has not always been a rewarding experience since it is difficult to achieve beautiful even Buttonhole Stitch. However, you can work perfect Buttonhole Stitch on canvas because the even weave of the mesh regulates the spacing and the height of the stitch. As a result of practice on canvas, you will achieve an equally fine Buttonhole Stitch on any fabric. Here are a few basic rules to get started. Work left to right. Come out at the lower edge where you want the festoon edge (scalloped edge). Never start in a corner. For crisp, well-defined stitches, use a twisted thread such as pearl cotton. Work over any reasonable number of canvas threads, usually 2, 3, 4, or 5.

Start by emerging one mesh opening to the left of the first stitch. Hold the thread with your thumb, go in at the top between the next 2 canvas threads, and come out directly below, with the needle over the working thread. Continue to go in at the top and to emerge at the base over a festoon (240).

When working Buttonhole edging around a shape, you will need to connect the last stitch to the first. Here is the way to accomplish this without a noticeable join: Do not work the last stitch in the normal fashion. Instead, slide the needle under the unoccupied festoon, made when starting the first Buttonhole Stitch. Then simply enter the top mesh opening and fasten off securely on the back of the work (241). In starting a freestanding row, emerge at the base of the stitch between 2 vertical canvas threads and enter the top mesh opening. Emerge a second time from the base, passing the needle over the festoon (242).

If you run out of thread in working Buttonhole Stitch, unthread the needle and let the thread dangle on the front of the canvas. With new thread, emerge from the last festoon, the same one from which the thread is dangling, and continue to stitch as though it were the old thread. Later, thread the needle with the dangling thread end, feed it back into the festoon, and secure it carefully on the back (243).

Turn a corner neatly, with the festoons on either the inside or the outside edge. Work an extra oblique Buttonhole Stitch between the corner mesh opening and all the mesh openings around the outer edge (244).

Use Double Buttonhole Stitch for a strong, textured line. Work a row of Buttonhole in the normal way, turn the work upside down, and enter a second row over and into the first row, inserting the needle into the festoons of the first row (245).

Add a Straight Gobelin between each Buttonhole Stitch for smooth, dense coverage. With the festoons at the top, emerge at the base and enter a festoon to the right of each Buttonhole Stitch (246).

Work a Buttonhole Eyelet as any Eyelet Stitch, but with festoons either in the mesh opening or around the outside edge. Enlarge the center opening first with an awl or rug needle. Close the Eyelet as described in 241 (247).

Create an open lacy effect on canvas (needle lace) by working one row of Buttonhole Stitch into another; you can also turn corners with this method: Skip a space between each stitch and drop 1 canvas thread between rows. From the second row, enter the first row over the festoon and a canvas thread (248).

Spaced Buttonhole or Blanket Stitch is another useful variation of Buttonhole Stitch. Simply vary the height of the stitch and/or the space between the stitches (249).

The technique of Couching is discussed later in this section, but here is an amusing way to couch down with Buttonhole Stitch. Use a highly decorative heavy thread, such as chenille, gold cord, or a wild knitting yarn. Dangle a length of it above the canvas and let the end fall gently into a swirl. Poke it with your needle into a handsome mass. Tie it down with freely worked Buttonhole Stitch (250).

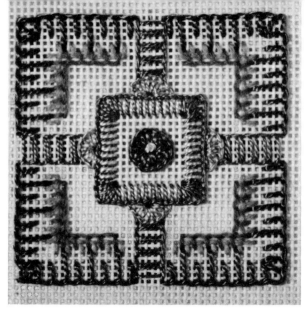

Symmetrical design, using sizes 3 and 5 pearl cotton and 2-ply Nantucket Twist. On 13-mesh.

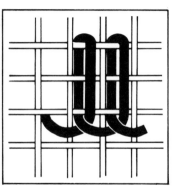

240. Emerge 1 to the left, leaving a vacant space. Enter at top, emerge again directly below, with needle over the festoon.

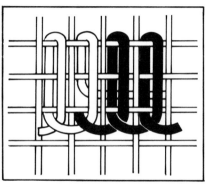

241. Join the last stitch to the first one by passing under the vacant festoon and entering the back at the top of the stitch.

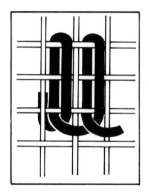

242. To start a Buttonhole Stitch with a straight edge, emerge twice from the same opening.

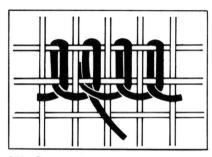

243. Start a new thread by letting the old one dangle from a festoon. Emerge from the same festoon and continue to stitch. Later, feed dangling end into the back of the work.

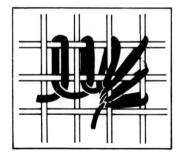

244. Turn a corner with all stitches emerging from the same opening; occupy all openings around the corner.

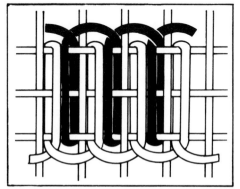

245. Double Buttonhole is worked in 2 journeys. The second journey is worked from the opposite side and enters the festoons of the first journey.

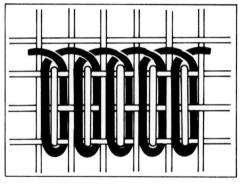

246. Satin Stitch into the festoons from right to left, with festoons at the top.

(continued)

(Buttonhole Stitch, *continued*)

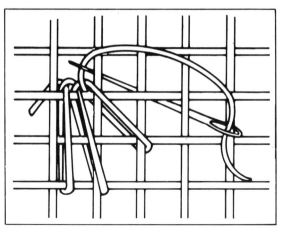

247. Produce Buttonhole Eyelets with festoons around the center mesh opening. Festoons can also be worked around the perimeter. Enlarge the center mesh opening first with an awl or rug needle.

Buttonhole Eyelet with festoons on the outside, in the center of swatch. Frame is Buttonhole and Satin Stitch. Four Half Buttonhole Eyelet with Buttonhole Stitch bars radiate from 4 sides of the frame. Spaced Buttonhole Stitch borders the swatch; needle lace embellishes the inside 4 corners.

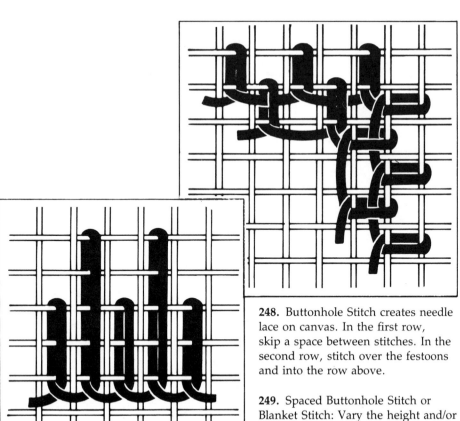

248. Buttonhole Stitch creates needle lace on canvas. In the first row, skip a space between stitches. In the second row, stitch over the festoons and into the row above.

249. Spaced Buttonhole Stitch or Blanket Stitch: Vary the height and/or the space between the stitches to create interesting patterns.

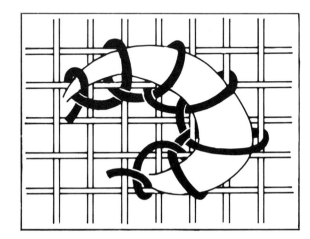

250. Use freely worked Buttonhole Stitch to couch interesting fibers in fanciful patterns.

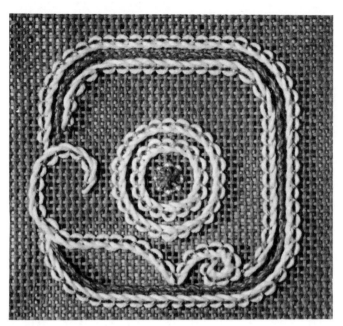

Pekinese Stitch, using size 5 pearl cotton for Back Stitch and
Cairo matte cotton for interlacing and for Outline Stem Stitch.
On tan 13-mesh.

Tied Double Cross Stitch is centered in 2 circles of joined
Pekinese Stitch. Graceful curving lines are achieved by
working Outline Back Stitch with oblique stitches as the
first journey for Pekinese and Outline Stem Stitch.

Pekinese Stitch

Pekinese Stitch is an ancient Chinese embroidery stitch; a
beautiful braid is produced by interlacing Back Stitch. Use
Pekinese for a textured outline, or work rows of it as a filling.
Use the same thread for the Back Stitch and the interlacing,
or for more drama, use a fine thread for the Back Stitch and a
slightly heavier one in another color for the interlacing.

Work Back Stitch in either direction, but work the interlacing
only from left to right. Do not draw the Back Stitch up tightly
as you must pass the needle under it without entering the
canvas.

When working a circle or a closed border, join the first and
last stitch imperceptibly: Come out from under the first Back
Stitch, hold the thread with your thumb to make a festoon
(scallop), slide the needle under the third Back Stitch, leave a
small loop at the top, and slide the needle down under the
second Back Stitch. Pass the needle over the festoon at the
bottom and release your thumb. Continue in this manner,
sharing each Back Stitch with 2 loops (251).

If you are not joining the first and last stitch, start by
emerging from the first Back Stitch and slide the needle up
under the second. (See Pekinese Stitch on the Sashiko Quilted
Vest front, on the canvas side, around a flower.)

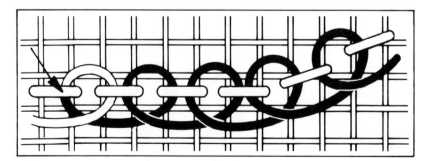

251. Emerge from the first Back Stitch. Hold a festoon, pass under the
third Back Stitch. Leave a small loop and pass down under the second Back
Stitch, over the festoon. Two loops share each Back Stitch.

143

Chain Stitch

Chain Stitch is another embroidery stitch adopted from non-counted thread work by needlepointers. Chain Stitch is most easily worked in vertical rows. Use oblique stitches to turn curves gradually (see Oblique Back Stitch), or turn them freely without precise stitch count.

Work Chain Stitch between 2 vertical canvas threads and over 2 horizontal canvas threads. Emerge from a mesh opening, hold the thread with your thumb, and reenter the same opening. Bring the needle out 2 canvas threads below, over the held thread, and draw up a Chain (252). Reenter the same opening, holding the thread in a loop, and emerge 2 canvas threads below (253).

Close Chain Stitch by entering a mesh opening 1 canvas thread below the emerging point, tying down the loop. To work a single Chain or a Detached Chain, work a Chain and close it as just described for the end of a row (254).

To keep stitches very even and to better see the point of entry, do not draw up the Chain until you insert the needle for the next stitch. Then, with the needle in a perpendicular position, draw the Chain up snugly against the needle.

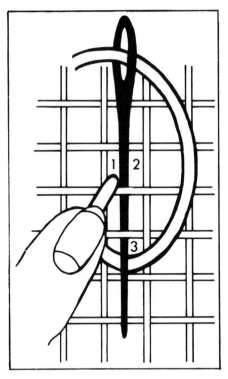

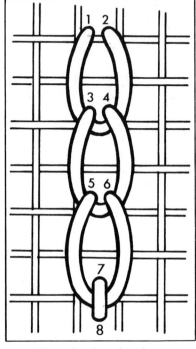

252. Emerge and reenter same opening; holding the Chain, emerge again 2 threads below, with loop under needle.

253. When the thread is drawn up, it catches the loop, and the first chain is made. Each Chain is held down by the one that follows it.

Chain Stitch, using 2-ply Persian. Log Cabin design worked by changing direction of stitches. Braided rug effect in center worked in a continuous Chain. On 12-mesh.

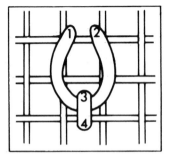

254. To close a row or to work a Detached Chain Stitch, enter 1 mesh opening beyond the emerging point.

144

Padded Satin Stitch

Satin Stitch is a Straight or Slanted Gobelin Stitch. Padded Satin, with its smooth, raised, light-reflecting surface, is a welcome addition to canvas work. Use it only for small areas, such as flower petals, because very long stitches are apt to snag or pull. Select thread that will lay flat and reflect light, such as cotton or silk floss.

Padded Satin is built up in layers. First work a Back Stitch outline, then fill the shape with Tent Stitch, slanting in the direction of the Satin to come (255). Gradually raise the surface: Work a layer of Satin over the Tent, leaving a row of Tent stitch exposed around the edge (256). Then with a full needle of carefully separated plies, lay Satin Stitch to cover the entire shape, including the Back Stitch. It is important that all plies of thread are laid in perfect alignment (257). Work Padded Satin in any direction, including oblique, horizontal, and vertical. (See a Padded Satin flower in section I1 of Fan Sampler.)

Padded Satin petals, using French silk; 2-ply for outline, 7-ply for Tent and Satin. Canvas Lace in flower center, using 1-ply sewing silk. Background, using 3-ply Nantucket Twist. Back Stitch, 2-ply silk. On tan 14-mesh.

Flower center is Canvas Lace. Each Cross Stitch is worked individually. Padded Satin petals slant to left, right, and oblique. Background is Rep Stitch worked diagonally, with Back Stitch added later between rows. Padded Satin border over 2 and 3 canvas threads with Oblong Cross in corners.

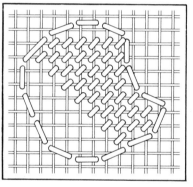

255. Outline with Back Stitch, fill with Tent.

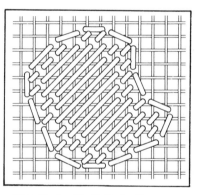

256. Pad with Satin in the center.

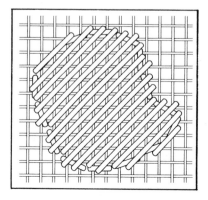

257. Enclose the entire shape with Satin.

Couching

Couching is a system for tying down a bulky laid thread with a second workable thread. Couch down, using any of the decorative stitches, such as Cross (258), Straight Gobelin (259), Herringbone (260), and Buttonhole (250). Or use short straight stitches that are perpendicular to the laid threads (261). Do not cut the laid thread in advance; cut it just once when you are almost finished.

To start Couching, feed the end of the laid thread through a large-eyed chenille needle. Sink the needle through a mesh opening, leaving a very short tail on the back of the work. With a sharp needle and sewing thread, tack this short end down in the direction of the Couching. An inch away from completion, cut and sink the laid thread into the back and tack it down, as you did to start. (See Couching in Flower Pictures I and II.)

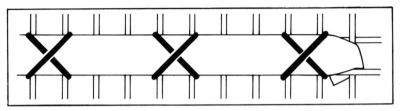

258. Couch down Ultrasuede or ribbon with Cross Stitch.

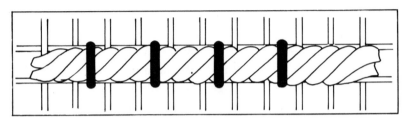

259. Couch down a heavy cord with Straight Gobelin, using fine matching thread.

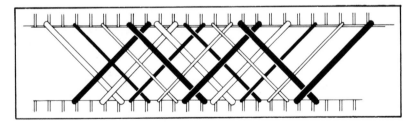

260. Couch down a wide ribbon or several narrow ones with Herringbone.

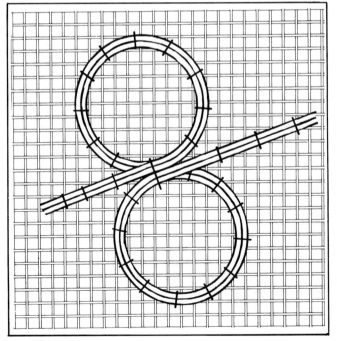

261. Couch down 2 strands of matte cotton, using 1 strand of finer matching thread, with straight stitches, perpendicular to the laid thread.

Underside Couching

Underside Couching is a system for laying an unbroken line of textured thread, such as chenille, on the canvas surface, and then tying it down with nooselike invisible Couching stitches.

At the right of the row, sink and fasten the thread to be laid, as described under Couching. Use strong, fine thread for Couching, such as linen or waxed silk, and a fine tapestry needle. Hold the laid thread down firmly with the left hand along the line to be worked. Bring the couching thread to the front, from a mesh opening about 4 canvas threads away from where the laid thread emerges. Pass over the laid thread and reenter the same mesh opening. Give the Couching thread a firm tug, pulling a bit of the laid thread to the underside (262). Continue in this manner, spacing the Couching stitches evenly.

On the back of the work, the Couching stitches will appear in a long straight line, and the laid thread will look like a little Running Stitch (263). (See Underside Couching in Flower Pictures I and II.)

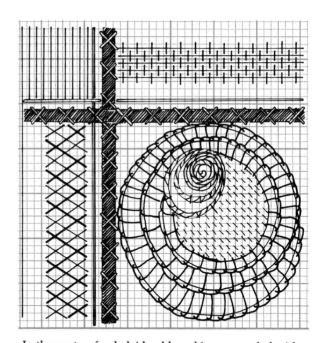

In the center, freely laid gold cord is surrounded with freely laid chenille and couched down with freely worked Buttonhole Stitch. Also in the center is an area of Tent Stitch, overlaid with blending filament. Underside Couching fills a square in the corner. Bokhara Couching is at the top of the swatch, and several rows of ribbon are couched down with Herringbone at the side. Gold cord is couched down with Straight Gobelin and Ultrasuede with Cross Stitch.

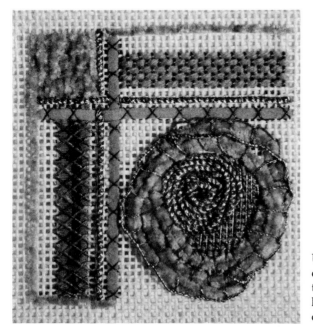

Ultrasuede, ribbon, gold cord, chenille, and matte cotton are laid and couched down with silk sewing thread, Brilliant Cutwork and Embroidery Thread, linen, blending filament, and fine gold cord. On linen canvas 13-mesh.

262. A heavy textured thread is laid, then a fine thread emerges from a mesh opening, encircles the heavy one, and reenters the mesh opening, pulling some of the heavy laid thread through the opening.

263. A side view showing the underside. The Couching thread appears as a straight line and the laid thread as a Running Stitch.

Bokhara Couching

Bokhara Couching produces an excellent background that looks like a woven fabric. In this Couching system you lay a thread and then overcast back over it with a return journey, completing each row in two steps. Always work from the top of the canvas down.

You can work Bokhara Couching in several ways. Here is the simplest method: Lay a thread from left to right between 2 canvas threads. Overcast back over the laid thread and over 2 canvas threads, skipping every other mesh opening. Note in diagram 264 how the laid thread moves to become the overcasting thread. Lay the thread for the second row as for the first. Overcast back between the overcasts of the first row in bricklike fashion. Every other row is alike.

A variation is to use 2 needles and 2 colors. Use 1 color for the laid thread; park the needle above the work. With the second needle traveling in the same direction, overcast the laid thread. Work the next row traveling in the opposite direction, laying the thread with one color, then overcasting back with the other, again in bricklike fashion. Alternate the rows (265). (See this variation in section A3 of Fan Sampler.)

Another method is to lay a thread from left to right between 2 canvas threads, and then overcast back over 3 canvas threads, skipping 2 mesh between the overcasts. Compensating stitches are worked in advance to produce a straight edge. Note diagram 266. In the first row, overcast back over only 1 canvas thread, skipping 2 mesh openings. In the second row, overcast back over 2 canvas threads, skipping the next 2 mesh openings. In the third row, start overcasting back over 3 canvas threads. A variation is to use 2 colors and 2 needles, as described above.

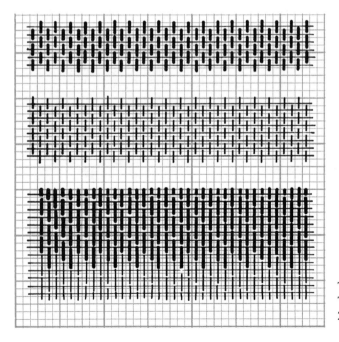

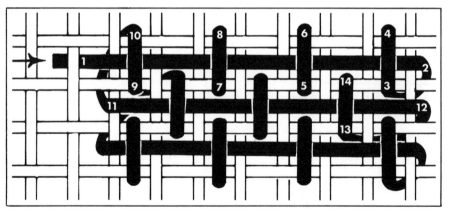

264. Lay thread left to right. Overcast back over 2 canvas threads, skipping 1 space between each overcast. After laying thread for next row, overcast back between overcasts in the row above.

Top band is worked in 2 colors, as in diagram 265.
The second band is worked in 1 color, as in diagram 264. The last 2 bands are worked as in diagram 266.

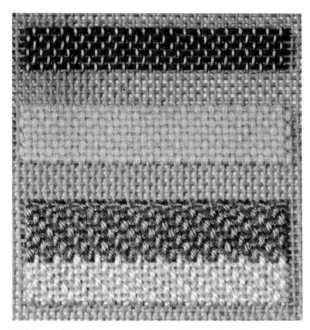

Bokhara Couching, using 2-ply Nantucket Twist, size 16 Brilliant Embroidery and Cutwork Thread, and size 3 pearl cotton. On tan 13-mesh.

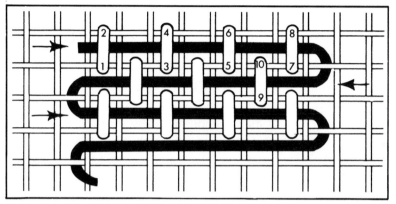

265. Use 2 needles and 2 colors. Lay thread left to right with first color. Park needle. Overcast laid thread with second color, from left to right. Park needle. Lay thread from right to left. Park needle. Etc.

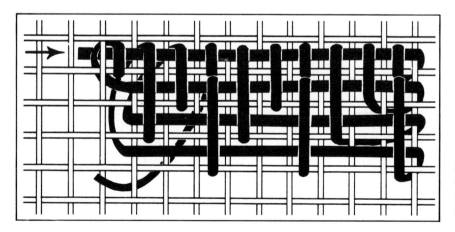

266. Bokhara Couching over 3 canvas threads. Skip 2 spaces between overcasts. Note compensation in first and second rows.

Canvas Beadwork

Canvas Beadwork is an inspiring Victorian legacy that is rather difficult to duplicate today because the same size bead in its subtle opaque neutral colors is just not readily available. If you are lucky enough to obtain some of this treasure, use a double mesh, or a very fine single mesh, covering 2 by 2 canvas threads. Experiment with canvas size to find the perfect fit for bead to canvas. Today only glass beads, classified as seed beads, are readily available in a range of strong, clear colors.

Work across a row, changing color within the row, as needed for the pattern. Use a long strand of tan sewing silk doubled through a size 8 or 10 sharp needle; wax the thread well. Use a Half Cross Stitch with snug tension. Stitch through the beads at both ends of each row twice to maintain a neat edge (267). (See Canvas Beadwork in section I of Fan Sampler and in Flower Pictures I and II.)

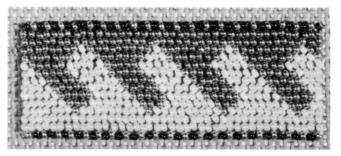

Design copied from an 1875 *Harper's Bazaar* magazine. Change bead colors as you travel across the row.

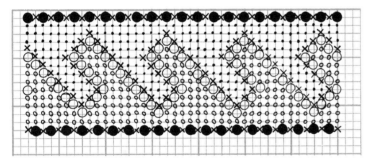

Glass seed beads stitched with tan sewing silk, doubled and waxed. On tan 13-mesh.

●	Black
✕	Old gold
•	Old rose
⊕	Cream
○	Pink

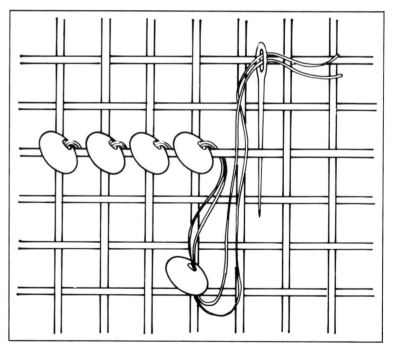

267. Use Half Cross, traveling left to right. Fasten bead down twice at the beginning and end of each row.

French Knot, French Knot on Stem

French Knot is very valuable for its "knotty" texture, which is unlike that of any other stitch. You will need both hands to work it, so a stretched canvas is important.

Emerge from a mesh opening. With your right hand, hold the needle parallel to the canvas. Wind the thread around the needle once or twice. Hold the thread firmly with the left hand (268). Rotate the needle to a perpendicular position, ready for a tent stitch. Hold the knot with the left hand (269). Draw the needle through snugly but not so firmly as to draw the knot through the opening.

French Knot on Stem is worked as a regular French Knot except that the needle enters a distant mesh opening (270). (See French Knot on Stem in section I1 of Fan Sampler.)

Note diagram 271 showing three French Knot variations.

French Knot and French Knot on Stem, using Swedish linen thread and chenille needle. Stitched through 12-mesh Zweigart Rustic Canvas with green fabric under it.

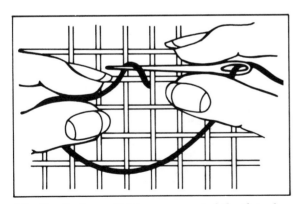

268. Needle is parallel to canvas; wind the thread once or twice.

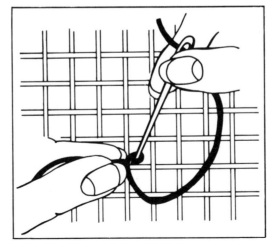

269. Rotate needle to perpendicular position. Hold the knot and enter, as for a Tent Stitch.

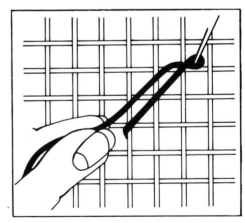

270. Same as 269 except that the needle enters a mesh opening at a distance.

(continued)

151

(French Knot, *continued*)

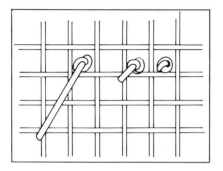

271. French Knot on Stem can slant in any direction. French Knot sits on an intersection, or on a mesh opening, providing the working thread is heavier than the canvas thread.

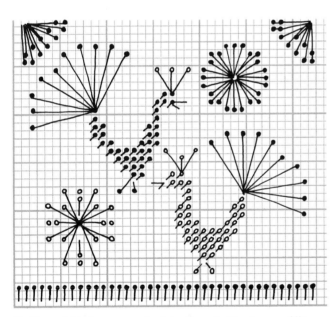

Bodies of birds are worked in French Knot as a filling. French Knot on Stem is used for the remainder of the design.

Bullion Knot

Bullion Knot looks like a short length of tightly twisted cord. To practice this stitch use a long thin needle and unstretched canvas. Once mastered, Bullion Knot can easily be worked on a stretched canvas as well.

Emerge opposite the desired closing point. Draw thread through, enter the closing point, and emerge once again at the starting point; do not draw thread through (272). Holding needle at the eye with one hand, wind the thread around tip end in the opposite direction the thread itself is twisted. Wind as many times as required to cover the distance between points of exit and entry (273). Coax needle through coiled thread with one hand, holding coils with the other. Adjust coils (274). Complete the Bullion Knot by entering closing point and emerging in position for next knot (275). Add extra winds for higher Bullion Knot loops.

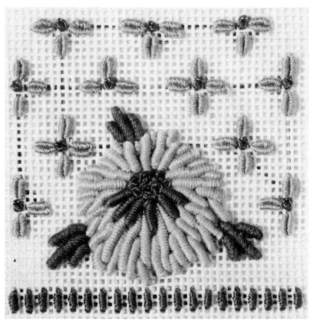

Large Bullion Knot flower, using cotton floss, full ply; leaves, using Cairo matte cotton; repeat pattern and border, using size 5 pearl cotton. On 13-mesh.

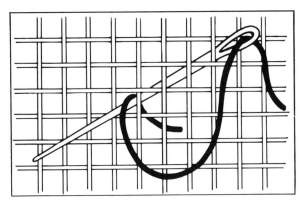

272. Emerge opposite the closing point; enter a distance away; emerge as before.

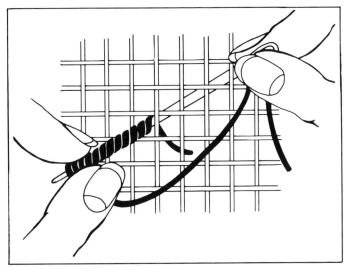

273. Wind thread in opposite direction of thread twist, as many times as needed to fill the length between exit and entry points.

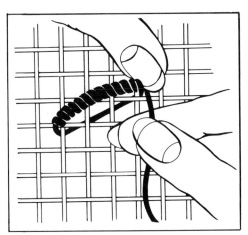

274. Coax needle through and draw up thread; adjust coils.

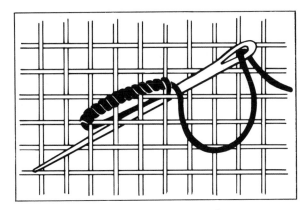

275. Reenter and emerge for the next knot.

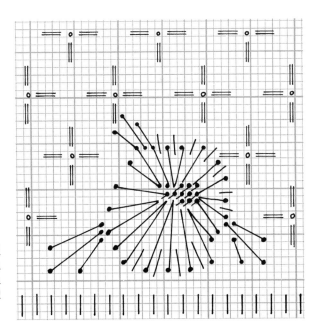

Outer petals are worked first in Bullion Knot, wound 15 to 25 times. Work other 2 layers, then work French Knot in center. In repeat pattern, pairs of Bullion Knot share mesh openings. A French Knot is worked in center of each small flower.

153

Spider Web

Spider Web is composed of needlewoven spokes that radiate from or across a center mesh opening. You can produce any number of spokes of any length, vary the kind of weaving, and even produce sections of a web.

Start with a simple web, with an even number of spokes, as in diagram 276, and needleweave a ribbed wheel: Emerge 1 opening below the center and to the right of spoke 13. Travel around the spokes, passing back over 1 and forward under 2, as though taking Back Stitch. Work a reverse ribbed wheel, as in diagram 277. Emerge to the left of 13 and pass forward over 2 and back under 1.

You can needleweave around an odd number of spokes by simply passing over 1 and under 1 (278). It is also possible to weave around just 4 spokes (279). Both half-web (280) and quarter-web (see swatch) are handsome worked in shaded pearl cotton with tips of some of the spokes left unworked.

You can eliminate the emphatic center opening by working spokes that cross each other. This results in a much more raised Spider Web (281). Note the many variations in the swatch. (See Spider Web in section A2 of Fan Sampler.)

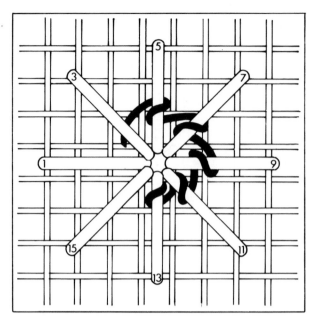

276. Spokes converge in center mesh opening. Pass back over 1 and forward under 2 for a ribbed wheel.

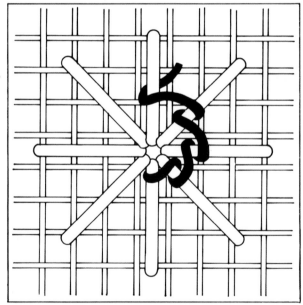

277. Pass forward over 2 and back under 1 to produce a reverse rib.

Spider Web variations scattered like stars, using sizes 3 and 5 pearl cotton; sizes 12 and 16 Brilliant Embroidery and Cutwork Thread. On 14-mesh.

154

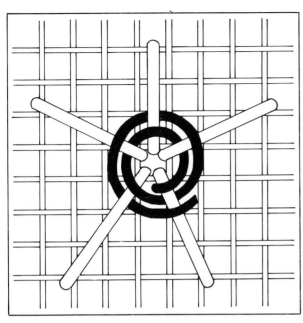

278. Pass over and under 1 to produce a woven wheel.

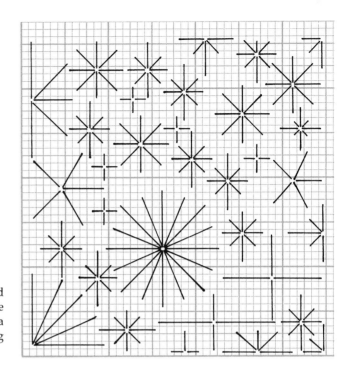

Many different sizes and numbers of spokes are used as framework for a variety of needleweaving techniques.

279. Use as many or as few spokes as you want. Produce a ribbed cross with 2 long spokes and 2 shorter ones.

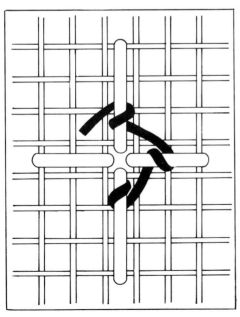

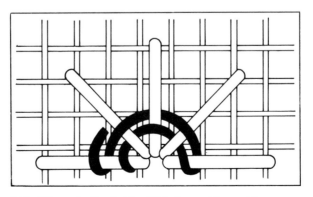

280. Weave half a Spider Web from side to side.

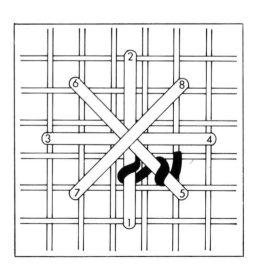

281. Cross the spokes without a center opening, using the same weaving methods. The result is a more raised Spider Web.

155

Detached Needleweaving

Detached needleweaving consists of warps that are first laid and then needlewoven above the canvas surface. You must stretch your canvas on wood stretcher bars for this process and you will need a tack for each warp. Establish a loom by hammering the tacks partway into the stretcher bar, in the general direction of the intended needleweaving. Thread a needle with a long length of thread, even the ends, draw half of this doubled thread through a mesh opening at the base of the work (282). Cut the thread at the eye, leaving 2 pairs of equal length thread. Wind each thread snugly around the shank of a tack and hammer the tack securely in place. With new thread, emerge from the base and start to needleweave, passing over and under the warps (283).

To shape a leaf or petal, start to needleweave very snugly, gradually loosening the tension to add breadth to the leaf. As you approach the tip, gradually tighten the tension. When you arrive at the tip, release the warps. Hold them in your left hand, place the needleweaving in a pleasing position, and sink the threaded needle into the back of the work. Pull it taut and secure it behind the work. Thread a needle with the 4 warps; sink and secure them (284).

To shape a calyx or anything requiring more warps, add more tacks, use more warps, and needleweave across all of them until it is time to divide them. Then needleweave one section at a time, fastening on a new thread at the base for each section (285). (See Detached Needleweaving in section I1 of Fan Sampler.)

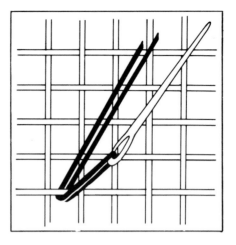

282. Draw half a doubled thread through at the base.

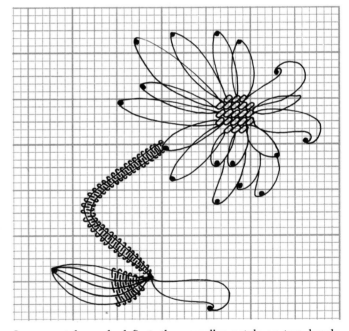

Larger petals worked first, then smaller petals on top, beads in center. Stem is needlewoven with 2 warps, petals and leaves with 4 warps.

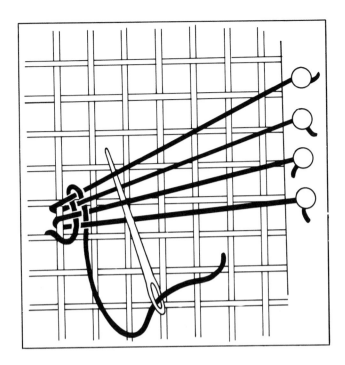

283. Create a loom with these threads as warps. Shape a leaf or petal by varying the tension of the needleweaving.

Detached Needleweaving, using Medicis crewel wool, Natesh rayon, Cairo matte cotton, and seed beads. On 14-mesh.

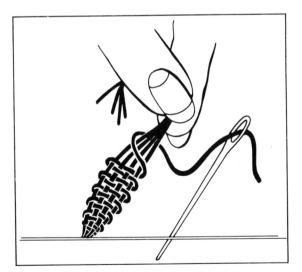

284. Release the needleweaving, place it in position, sink and fasten it down under the work. Sink the warps and secure them.

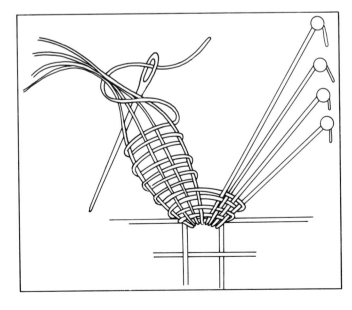

285. Use as many warps as needed; divide when necessary. Complete each new section, then resume where the weaving was left off.

Projects

A group of fascinating sampler projects
designed to make learning fun

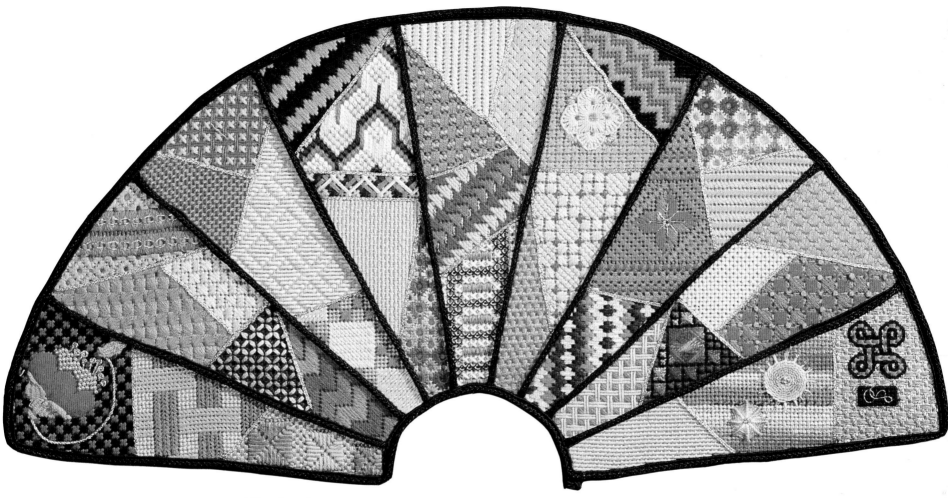

Fan Sampler

A classic Japanese fan shape displays exciting needlepoint stitch patterns within its divided space. The finished work is mounted as a textile sculpture. The fan itself measures 17 inches at its widest point and 8½ inches in height, finished size.

Patchwork Sampler I

Beginner's 3-x-3-inch sample swatches find an attractive home when assembled into a quilted wall hanging.

Patchwork Sampler II

Samples of more advanced stitches are sewn into a second wall hanging. Each hanging measures 20 x 23 inches, finished size.

Patchwork Pillow

Another suggested use for study swatches is this cheerful pillow. Chair pads, footstools, even headboards, are other possibilities. What a virtuous way to use up leftover canvas and yarns!

Geometric Designs

These designs stitched in wool are ideal for upholstering. They can be worked by anyone who can follow a graph.

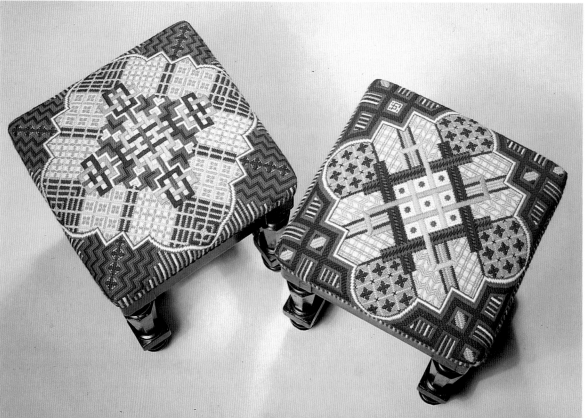

Sashiko Quilted Reversible Vest

A vest, inspired by Japanese folk embroidery, suitable to be worn day or night, year in and year out. It is stitched in matte cotton through two layers, a tan 18-mesh canvas on top and black cotton fabric underneath. The counted stitches worked on the canvas side (seen in the illustrations above) make handsome even stitching on the darker fabric side (seen in the illustrations below). Black and white lace and tiny buttons add festive touches to the dark fabric. I don't know which has been more enjoyable, to make this vest or to wear it.

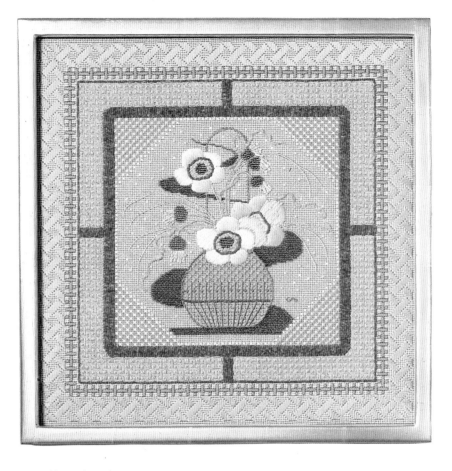

Silken Flower Pictures

These subtle and peaceful pictures employ many highly textured stitches in both the flowers and the baskets. Worked entirely in silk, the stitches change in direction and play with the reflection of light. Beads and chenille add further interesting texture. The unframed pictures measure approximately 16 inches square, finished size.

Alphabet Samplers.

Here is yet another way to learn and practice a wide variety of stitches. Alphabet letters can be combined with other designs to enhance tote bags, pictures, and pillows or used alone in an alphabet picture, quilt, or other projects.

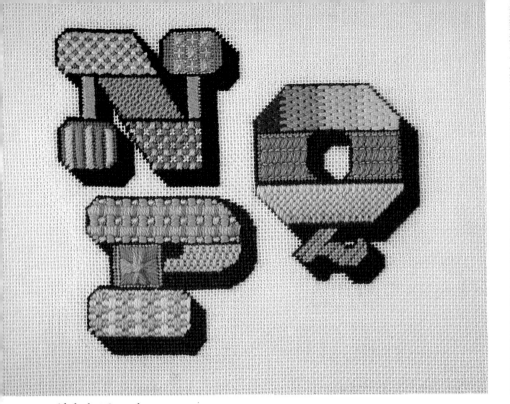

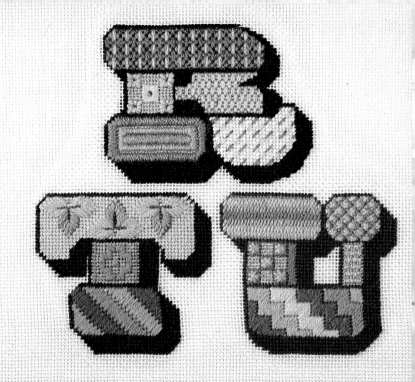

Alphabet Samplers

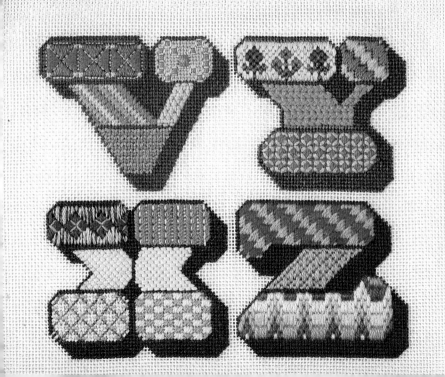

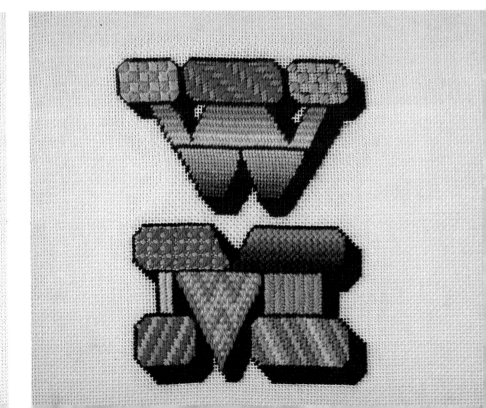

Materials Used to Work Fan

All threads are listed by number. In the Guide to Fan Stitches and Threads these same numbers, in **boldface italic,** are used to refer to these threads. In some cases a second or third choice of thread is offered as a substitute, but the first-mentioned thread is the one that is actually used.

The tan canvas on which the fan is worked is Zweigart, deluxe quality, 13-mesh. It is cut 13 × 22 inches and mounted on a stretcher bar frame of the same dimensions. Needles are sizes 20, 22, 24 tapestry; size 22 chenille. Sharp needle, size 8, and beeswax are used for the beadwork. The finished, mounted fan measures 17 inches at its widest point and 8½ inches in height.

Threads

A wide variety of thread textures and colors adds richness to the fan's many stitch patterns.

1 Silk, black, Soie d'Alger (the brand name is Au Ver A Soie), or DMC floss

2 Silk, light peach, Soie d'Alger 931, or DMC floss 353

3 Silk, dark peach, Soie d'Alger 933, or DMC floss 352

4 Silk, fuchsia, Soie Crystale 2318, or Soie d'Alger 1034, or DMC floss 603

5 Silk, light purple, Soie Crystale 2369, or Soie d'Alger 1324, or DMC floss 553

6 Silk, light periwinkle blue, Soie Crystale 2379, or Soie d'Alger 1434, or DMC floss 341

7 Silk, light aqua, Soie Crystale 2374, or Soie d'Alger 132, or DMC floss 598

8 Silk, dark aqua, Soie Crystale 2372, or Soie d'Alger 134, or DMC floss 958

9 Gold Blending Filament, Balger, or DMC gold metallic thread

10 Gold Tinsel Thread, Lumiyarn, or either of the above

11 Gold braid or 1½ Lumiyarn, or Japan gold braid #8, Kreinik

12 Gold passing thread #5, Kreinik

13 Gold twisted cord, Torsade #5, Kreinik

14 Wool, peony pink 36, Nantucket Twist

15 Wool, lilac 46, Nantucket Twist

16 Wool, petunia 43, Nantucket Twist

17 Wool, chicory blue 55, Nantucket Twist

18 Wool, china blue 52, Nantucket Twist

19 Silk ribbon, ⅛" width, blue 81, Kanagawa

20 Matte cotton, butter 24, Cairo, or DMC floss 745

21 Matte cotton, scallion 85, Cairo, or DMC floss 966

22 Matte cotton, apple blossom 42, Cairo, or DMC floss 894

23 Matte cotton, dark green 2909, DMC

24 Brilliant Embroidery and Cutwork Thread, size 12, red 666, DMC

25 Brilliant Embroidery and Cutwork Thread, size 12, yellow 444, DMC

26 Pearl cotton, size 5, shaded pink-red 57, DMC

27 Pearl cotton, size 5, shaded orange, 108, DMC

28 Pearl cotton, size 5, light yellow 745, DMC

29 Pearl cotton, size 5, light orange 972, DMC

30 Pearl cotton, size 3, orange 740, DMC

31 Linen, green 334, Swedish Kulört Lingarn

32 Seed Beads, tangerine 423, Mill Hill Graphics

33 Rayon Soutache, flat ⅛" wide, black

34 Rayon braid, ⅛" round, black

35 Silk sewing thread, size A, black, Belding Corticelli

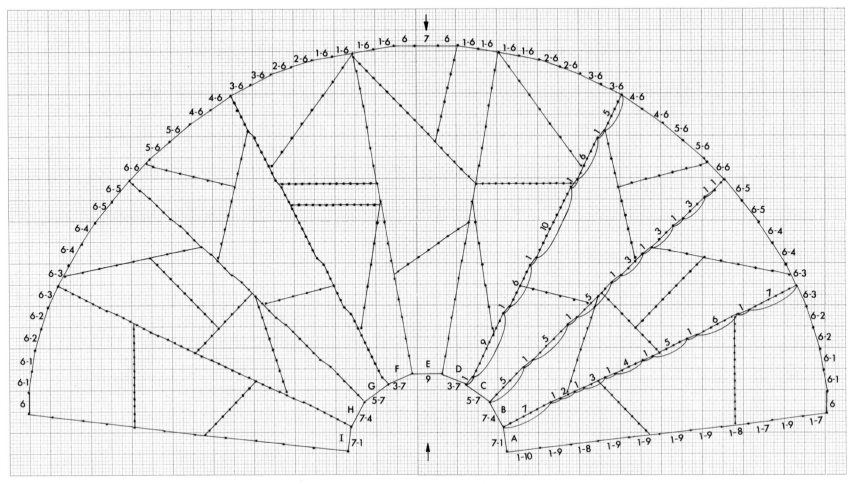

Start the work by backstitching the outline of the fan, the fins, and the segments.

Stitching the Fan

1. With black silk sewing thread and size 24 tapestry needle, backstitch the entire outline of the fan. Note the numbers around the perimeter: They are used to save counting. The first number indicates how many horizontal canvas threads to move over, up, or down; the second number indicates how many vertical threads to move over, either to left or right. Example: 6/1 means move the needle up over 6 canvas threads and over 1 horizontal thread.

2. With the same thread and needle, backstitch the dividing lines between the fins and the segments within them. Here the numbers indicate how many of each stitch count is made. Example: 2 means there are two identical stitches moving over the same number of canvas threads in each direction.

3. Work all the filling stitches following the Guide to Fan Stitches and Threads.

NOTE: The right and left sides of the fan are in mirror reverse. The only fins that do not match exactly are A and I, D and F. In fin I, the segments are slightly different in size than in A, and in fin F there is an extra segment for the Herringbone border.

Guide to Fan Stitches and Threads

Directions for working stitches shown in *italic* are found in the Dictionary of Stitches. The numbers in ***boldface italic*** placed after each stitch refer to the threads listed in Materials Used to Work Fan on page 161.

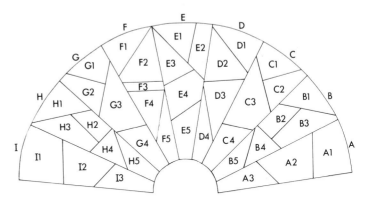

Each fin is identified with a letter; the segments within each fin, with a number.

A 1   Motif outlined in *Back Stitch*, 7-ply ***1***
       Motif filled with *Back Stitch*, 7-ply ***4***
       Rectangle ground for monogram, *Tent Stitch*, 7-ply ***1***
       Monogram laid with ***12***, *Couching*, ***10***
       Background pattern, *Darning*, ***11***, ***19***

A 2   *Spider Web*, 1-ply ***27***
       Centers, *French Knot* ***11***
       Blended ground, *Reversed Tent Stitch*, 7-ply ***4***, ***3***, ***2***, ***6***, ***7***, ***8***, ***5*** and 3-ply ***17***, ***46***

A 3   *Bokhara Couching*, ***21***, *couched* down with ***25***

B 1   *Diamond Ray Stitch*, 7-ply ***3***

B 2   *Alternating Tent Stitch*, ***20***

B 3   *Cushion Stitch*, 7-ply ***5***
       Back Stitch and French Knot, ***31***

B 4   *Rhodes Stitch*, the largest square and six medium-size squares, ***26***
       Smyrna Stitch, smallest squares, ***26***
       Back Stitch outline, 5-ply ***1***

B 5   *Bucky's Weaving, Cross Stitch*, 3-ply ***14***, and *Darning*, tightly twisted 7-ply ***6***

C 1   *Round Eyelet*, ***26***, alternating rows with *Diamond Eyelet*, ***29***

C 2   *Gobelin Stem Stitch*, 7-ply ***7***

C 3   *Leaf Stitch Medallion*, 7-ply ***4***, with center of 3-ply ***9***
       Continuous Mosaic, 7-ply ***8*** behind the medallion, edged top and bottom with tip of *Tip of Leaf Stitch*, 7-ply ***4***
       Parisian Stitch, 7-ply ***8*** and 7-ply ***4***, one row each above and below *Tip of Leaf Stitch*

C 4   *Hungarian Ground*, pairs of *Wave Stitch* rows, 4-ply ***18***, alternating with pairs in blend of ***25***, ***28***, ***29***
       Hungarian Stitch rows, 4-ply ***18***, ***17***, and blend of ***28***, ***29***, ***25***

D 1   *Jacquard Stitch*, rows of 3-ply ***15***, alternating with rows of 7-ply ***4***
       Kalem Stitch ground, 7-ply ***1***

D 2   Large *Square Eyelet*, ***25***
       Half *Buttonhole Stitch* eyelet, ***29***
       Quarter *Eyelet* in four corners ***30***
       Mosaic Stitch ground, ***31***

D 3   *Cushion Stitch* units, 7-ply ***6***, alternate with *Upright Cross Stitch* squares, ***29***
       Where corners of units meet, *Upright Cross Stitch*, 3-ply, ***16***
       Back Stitch on Cushion Stitch units, 1-ply ***17***

D 4   *Double and Tie Stitch*, 7-ply ***3***

E 1   *Gobelin Stem Stitch*, 7-ply ***6***

E 2   *Herringbone-Gone-Wrong*, 7-ply ***2***

E 3   *Parisian Stitch* long stitches, 7-ply ***8***, and short stitches, ***30***
       Back Stitch, horizontal rows, 7-ply ***8***

E 4   *Milanese Stitch* diagonal stripes of 3-ply ***16***, 7-ply ***4***, and ***22***
       Straight Gobelin Stitch, ***11***

E 5   *Canvas Lace Cross Stitch*, ***28***, and 1-ply ***1***, and *Darning*, ***19***

F 1   *Continuous Flat Stitch*, stripes, 7-ply ***1***, ***2***

F 2 *Bargello* pattern, rows of 4-ply **18, 17,** blend of **28, 29, 25,** 3-ply **25,** 3-ply **29**

F 3 *Herringbone Border,* 3-ply **18,** 7-ply **8,** blend of 1-ply **28** and 1-ply **25**

F 4 *Bokhara Couching,* **21,** couched down with **25**

F 5 *Round Eyelet,* **26,** alternating rows with *Diamond Eyelet,* **27**

G 1 *Bucky's Weaving, Cross Stitch,* 7-ply **22,** and *Darning,* tightly twisted **5**

G 2 *Bokhara Couching,* **30,** couched down with **24**

G 3 *Kogin* pattern, **20**

G 4 *Web Stitch* squares, 3-ply **6,** alternating with *Flat Stitch,* 7-ply **8,** and *Tent Stitch* squares, 7-ply **7**

H 1 *Shell Stitch,* 3-ply **17,** coils **9,** *Back Stitch* between rows, 5-ply **4.**
  Diamond Eyelet above and below, 7-ply **7**

H 2 *Flat Stitch* and *Cashmere Stitch* alternate, 7-ply **6**

H 3 *Ray Stitch,* 7-ply **3**

H 4 *Crossed Corners Stitch, Cross Stitch,* 3-ply **18,** corners crossed by **27**
  Back Stitch in vertical and horizontal rows, 1-ply **18**

H 5 *Byzantine Stitch,* alternate rows, 7-ply **5,** 3-ply **15,** and 3-ply **16**

I 1 *Padded Satin Stitch* flower, 7-ply **4**
  Canvas Beadwork, beads **32,** sewn with 2-ply **3**
  French Knot on Stem, **11**
  Calyx flower base and leaf, *Needleweaving,* **31**
  Stem, *Couching,* **13,** couched down with **10**
  Background, *Small Chequer Stitch,* composed of *Tent Stitch,* 7-ply **1,** and *Mosaic Stitch,* 7-ply **5**

I 2 *Kalem Stitch,* woven ribbon pattern, 7-ply **8** for verticals and 7-ply **7** for horizontals
  Small *Cross Stitch* ground, **25**

I 3 *Triangle Stitch,* **23,** and **31** for the largest and smallest squares
  Medium square, **21** and **31**
  All *Back Stitch,* **31**
  Brick Stitch background, 7-ply **2**
  Dividing lines within each fin, *Couching,* 2 strands **11,** couched down with **10**
  Dividing lines between fins, *Couching,* **33,** held with *Back Stitch,* **35,** overlaid with **34** couched down with **35**
  Outline of entire Fan Sampler, 2 rows **33,** overlaid with **34** couched down with **35**

Finishing and Mounting Fan

To mount the fan as a raised sculpture, as in the photograph in the color section of this book, add a three-quarter-inch band of Tent Stitch all around the outer edges using black wool. Note in the diagram that the corners are "stepped" to create a neat finish and that notches are left unstitched in the small convex curve.

Apply white acid-free glue to the underside of the unstitched notches, then slash them so they will fold back smoothly.

Stretch and fasten down the completed needlework over a fan-shaped piece of one-quarter-inch plywood that has been covered with museum board. As you will note in the photograph, the fan projects slightly from a silk rep-covered board. To accomplish this, a one-quarter-inch spacer (block of wood) should be fastened between the board and fan.

Graph for Stitching Fan

Each stitch pattern has a letter and number. See Guide to Fan Stitches and Threads. There you will find the stitch names and threads. The threads are listed on page 161, the stitches in the Dictionary of Stitches.

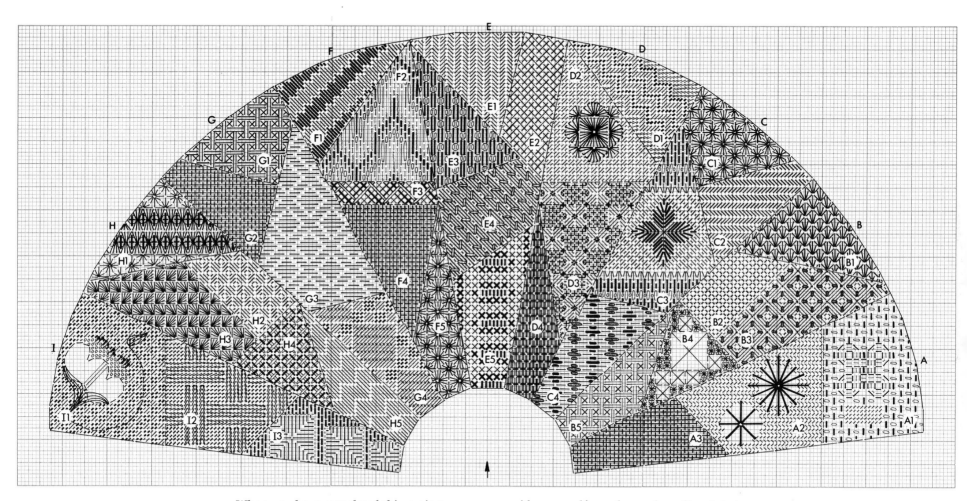

When you have completed this project you may consider yourself an advanced needlepointer!

Guide to Patchwork Samplers

1	2	3	4	5	6
7	8	9	10	11	12
13	14	15	16	17	18
19	20	21	22	23	24
25	26	27	28	29	30

1	2	3	4	5	6
7	8	9	10	11	12
13	14	15	16	17	18
19	20	21	22	23	24
25	26	27	28	29	30

1	2	3	4	5	6
7	8	9	10	11	12
13	14	15	16	17	18
19	20	21	22	23	24
25	26	27	28	29	30

PATCHWORK I STITCHES

1 Kalem
2 Continuous Flat
3 Jacquard
4 Mosaic
5 Florentine
6 Double Cross
7 Milanese
8 Tied Oblong Cross
9 Rococo
10 Parisian
11 Square Eyelet
12 Leaf
13 Straight Gobelin
14 Back
15 Shell
16 Oriental
17 Bargello
18 Triangle
19 Cashmere
20 Back
21 Chain
22 Triangle
23 Continuous Mosaic
24 Scottish
25 Cross
26 Large and Upright Cross
27 Hungarian
28 Cushion
29 Bargello
30 Straight Gobelin

PATCHWORK II STITCHES

1 Couching
2 Woven Band
3 Bullion Knot
4 Waffle
5 Padded Satin
6 Outline Back and Oblique Back
7 French Knot
8 Round Eyelet
9 Kogin
10 Diamond Eyelet
11 Ray
12 Sashiko
13 Bucky's Weaving
14 Spider Web
15 Pekinese
16 Buttonhole
17 Squared Herringbone
18 Crewel, Outline, and Alternating Stem
19 Square Eyelet
20 Diagonal Leaf
21 Leaf Stitch Medallion
22 Darning
23 Rhodes
24 Kogin, Sashiko, and Canvas Beadwork
25 Canvas Lace
26 Detached Needleweaving
27 Herringbone
28 Tied Double Cross
29 Bokhara Couching
30 Running

PATCHWORK PILLOW STITCHES

1 Triangle
2 Smyrna
3 Large and Upright Cross
4 Square Eyelet
5 Rococo
6 Bargello
7 Straight Gobelin
8 Continuous Mosaic
9 Tied Oblong Cross
10 Cross, Upright Cross, St. George and St. Andrew
11 Triple Cross
12 Mosaic
13 Kalem
14 Gobelin Stem
15 Hungarian
16 Triangle
17 Knotted
18 Large Chequer
19 Double Cross
20 Cushion
21 Crossed Corners
22 Scottish
23 Long-armed Cross
24 Oblong Cross
25 Back
26 Hungarian
27 Back
28 Bargello
29 Leaf
30 Parisian

Stitching the Samplers

Here is a splendid opportunity to use a variety of canvases and threads while learning new stitches and techniques. For each sampler use the above guides or select 30 stitches of your own choice from the Dictionary of Stitches. You can plan the colors, values, and placement for each square in advance for a well-organized effect, or you can just have fun and let the finished swatches direct their own placement.

The canvas mesh and the threads used in the patchwork samplers are noted under the black and white photographs of most stitch swatches in the Dictionary of Stitches.

Materials Used

In addition to various types of canvas, threads, and needles, you need two pairs of 6-inch stretcher bars for a frame on which to tack or tautly staple the small canvas squares. Cut all the canvas pieces 6 inches square. The needlework should measure exactly 3 inches square and be centered on the canvas squares. To mount the completed patchwork sampler as shown, you need a frame assembled from one pair of 20-inch artist's wide stretcher bars, and one 23-inch pair. In addition, you need two pieces of white cotton fabric, such as old sheeting, and one piece of thin quilt batting, all 25 × 28 inches, plus a little over a yard of calico printed fabric.

Assembling Swatches

1. Trim the stitch swatches, leaving one-half inch of bare canvas on all sides.

2. Overcast the raw edges by hand or zigzag them by machine.

3. Overlap and join groups of five swatches into six long strips, leaving one-half inch bare canvas between each square.

4. Cut long strips of calico print fabric, one and one-half inches wide. Fold and press the raw edges in to make a tape, one-half inch wide.

5. Cut the tape so that you have twenty-four pieces, each 3½ inches long, and five pieces, each 18 inches long.

6. Appliqué these short tapes by hand over the one-half-inch bare horizontal canvas joinings.

7. Overlap and join the long strips of swatches, leaving one-half-inch bare canvas between the strips.

8. Appliqué five 18-inch-long tapes over the vertical bare canvas joinings.

9. Cut two strips of calico fabric, 4 inches wide by 25 inches long. Cut two strips of calico fabric, 4 inches wide by 21 inches long.

10. Turn under the raw edges along one side of these strips and edge the assembled sampler with them, mitering the corners.

11. You can add a Victorian crazy quilt touch by outlining each square with embroidery stitches in pearl cotton. Try using Stem, Buttonhole, Herringbone, and Detached Chain stitches. This stitching camouflages any nonalignment of the squares.

12. Use the patchwork for a pillow front or as the wall hanging described below.

Mounting a Wall Hanging

1. Stretch a piece of the white cotton fabric over the whole framed space and around to the back of the frame; staple it down.

2. Stretch the batting over this and then stretch a second piece of white fabric over the batting. Staple both down on the back.

3. Stretch the sampler over the padded surface and staple the excess calico fabric down on the back.

4. You can now achieve a quilted effect, as seen in Sampler I in the color section, by taking tiny stitches at the intersections of the squares. Or, as in Sampler II, also as seen in the color section, you can stitch a Spider Web through the entire thickness at the intersections, adding a French Knot in the center of each web.

5. For a neat finish, hand tack a piece of calico fabric over the entire reverse side of the piece.

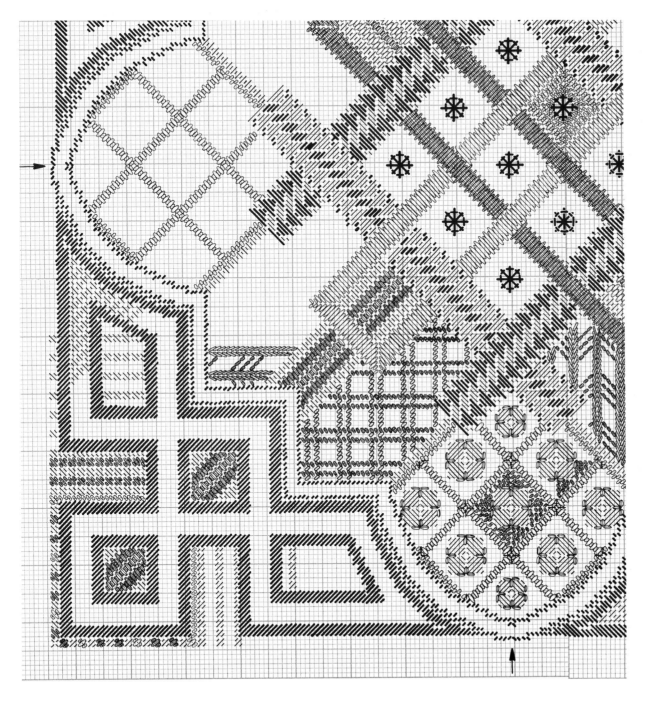

Graph for Geometric Design I

It is easy to follow both of these graphs by referring to Key to Threads and Key to Stitches. Note the arrows that point out the centers of the designs. Turn the work to complete all four corners. For the sake of visual clarity, portions of the graphs are left open. See a corresponding portion for the filling stitches. Consult the color photographs where you will see that some areas are worked in white.

Key to Threads for Both Pictures

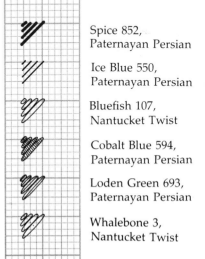

Spice 852,
Paternayan Persian

Ice Blue 550,
Paternayan Persian

Bluefish 107,
Nantucket Twist

Cobalt Blue 594,
Paternayan Persian

Loden Green 693,
Paternayan Persian

Whalebone 3,
Nantucket Twist

Graph for Geometric Design II

Key to Stitches for Both Pictures

 Tied Double Cross

 Continuous Mosaic

 Continuous Mosaic

 Long Diagonal

 Oriental

 Cushion

 Mosaic

 Kalem

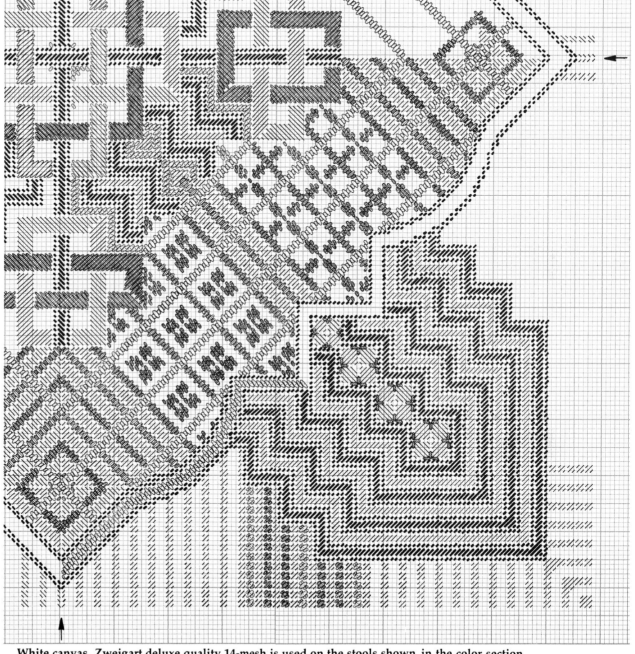

White canvas, Zweigart deluxe quality 14-mesh is used on the stools shown in the color section.

169

Materials Used to Work Vest

Dull matte cotton echoes the stringlike thread traditionally used for Japanese Sashiko and Kogin embroidery. Instead of the indigo blue fabric associated with this work, I have used a soft tan 16-mesh Congress Canvas whose texture is similar to even-weave Kogin material but more open. A black, soft cotton fabric, coarser than percale, was used as a backing. I used a cotton darner needle, with a stabbing up and down motion, to stitch with matte cotton, a size 22 chenille needle with a scooping motion, to stitch the Brilliant Embroidery and Cutwork Thread, and a sharp sewing needle and black thread for the appliqué work when I reversed the front and back fabrics. I chose a simple pattern, without darts, for the vest. Black and white lace, tiny black cloth buttons, and pink jewel buttons were all used as extra decorative touches on the black fabric side.

I did not put the work on a frame, but instead used a weighted pillow to hold the vest down as I stitched at my worktable. I used embroidery hoops when I stitched the flowers.

Below is a list of the threads used, all from DMC.

1 16 skeins matte cotton, article 89, wine 2902
2 7 skeins matte cotton, article 89, blue 2594
3 4 skeins matte cotton, article 89, peach 2356
4 3 skeins Brilliant Embroidery and Cutwork Thread, article 107, size 16, dark blue 516
5 3 skeins Brilliant Embroidery and Cutwork Thread, article 107, size 16, light blue 799
6 5 skeins Brilliant Embroidery and Cutwork Thread, article 107, size 12, black 310
7 2 skeins Brilliant Embroidery and Cutwork Thread, article 107, size 12, wine 902

Stitching the Vest: How to Get Started

1. If you plan to bind the outer edges of your vest with handmade or bought foldover braid, remove the seam allowances from the vest pattern pieces, but leave the shoulder seam allowance.

2. Pin the pattern pieces to the canvas.

3. Cut the canvas into rectangles that are two inches larger than the pattern pieces all around.

4. Bind the edges of the canvas with machine zigzag or hand overcast.

5. Cut matching rectangles of the black cotton fabric.

6. With light-colored thread, work a running stitch all around the pattern pieces.

7. Remove the pattern pieces.

8. With very large crisscross stitches, baste the two fabrics together to stabilize them.

9. Using dark blue Brilliant Embroidery and Cutwork Thread, backstitch the dividing lines for the stitch patterns. Follow the diagram showing the layout for Dividing Lines for Vest Stitch Patterns.

Dividing Lines for Vest Stitch Patterns

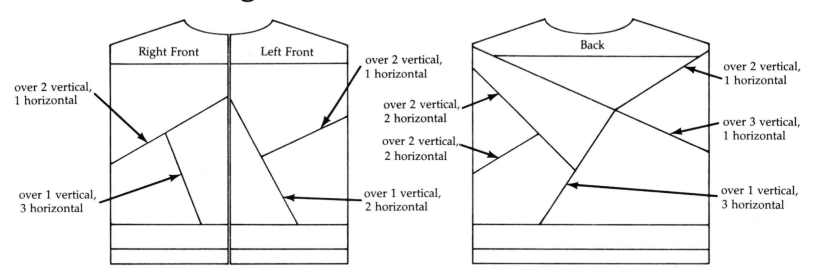

Divide the front and back of the vest into shapes to fill with different stitch patterns. To achieve dividing lines that angle in various degrees, work Back Stitch over canvas threads in each direction.

Reverse Appliqué

On each vest front and on the vest back, a layer of black fabric is applied over a divided area and the black fabric on the back is cut away. In other words, the canvas side will have some black shapes and the fabric side will have some canvas shapes.

This is how it is done: Make a tracing paper pattern of the shape and cut shapes from leftover black fabric one-quarter inch larger all around than the shapes they are to cover. Baste the shape into place. Turn under the raw edges; carefully and invisibly tack them down at the backstitched lines. Then turn the entire piece to the fabric side. Cut away the black fabric on the fabric side within the shape, leaving one-sixteenth-inch margins. Overcast the raw edges neatly along the Back Stitch outlines. Later, braid and lace will cover these edges.

Filling the Shapes

All of the stitching is done on the canvas side, which provides evenness to the stitching on the fabric side. To secure a working thread when starting, slide the needle under the canvas, between the two materials, about two inches away from the work in the direction you are stitching.

To secure a thread when ending off, slide the needle through some of the stitched channels and clip it very closely on the front.

Follow Guide to Vest Stitch Patterns to fill all the shapes. Kogin, Sashiko, Stem Stitch, Back Stitch, Cross Stitch, Darning, and Couching are described in the Dictionary of Stitches.

Guide to Vest Stitch Patterns

To fill the shapes, match the pattern numbers to the stitch patterns. The numbers in **_boldface italic_** following the illustration of the stitch patterns refer to the threads used. See the thread list under Materials Used to Work Vest, page 170.

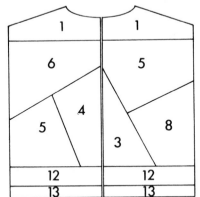

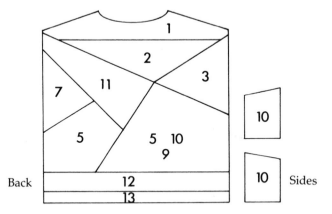

This guide drawing shows the stitch patterns from the canvas side only since most stitching is done on this side. However, stitch patterns 3, 4, and 11 are actually stitched on the canvas side but are shown on the fabric side because of the reverse appliqué.

See the photograph of the vest for color placement of threads. See Materials to Work Vest, where threads are identified by number.

All threads are used single ply except the stem of the large flower, where two strands of matte cotton are couched down at one time.

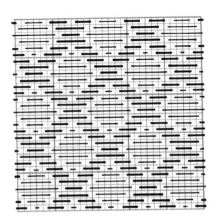

1. Kogin diamonds, **_1_**

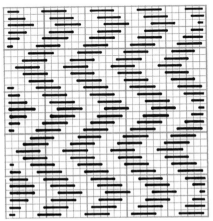

2. Kogin zigzag, **_7_**. Complete entire pattern, then feed extra thread through cores of zigzags to solidify stitches.

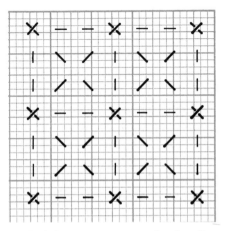

3. Sashiko squares, crossed twice, **_2_** and **_4_**

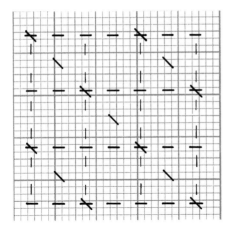

4. Sashiko squares, crossed once, **3** and **7**

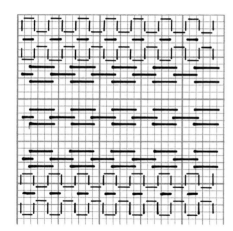

6. Kogin and Sashiko horizontal stripes, **2**, **3**, **5**, and **6**

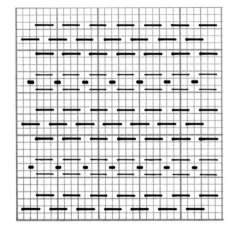

7. Kogin horizontal stripes, **2**, **3**, and **5**

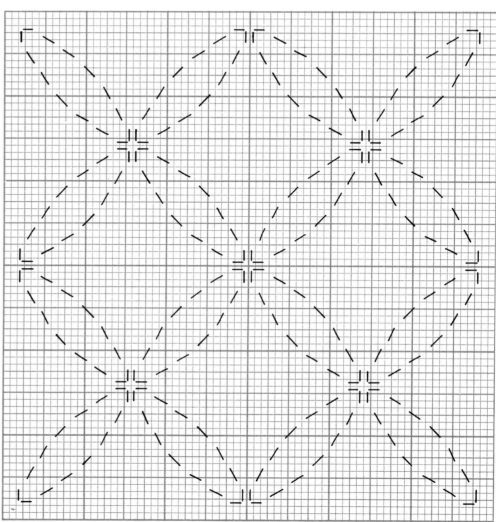

5. Sashiko connecting circles, **1**

173

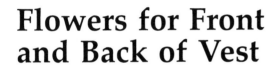

Flowers for Front and Back of Vest

These flowers are first worked freely in Back Stitch, then overstitched with Crewel and Outline Stem Stitch, Chain, Cross, Pekinese, and Couching.

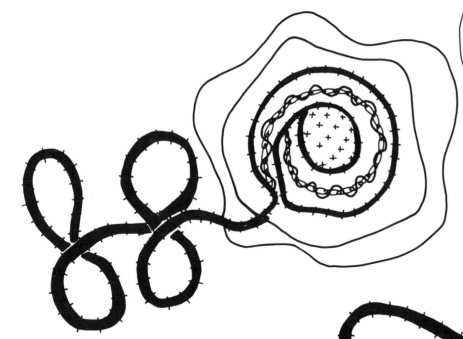

8. Small flower has a background of Kogin horizontal stripes, worked vertically, *1*, *3*, *4*, and *5*

9. Large flower has Sashiko diamonds on one side and Sashiko connecting circles on the other side, *1*, *3*, *4*, and *5*

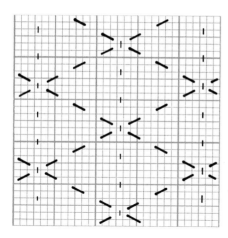

10. Sashiko diamonds, *2* and *3*

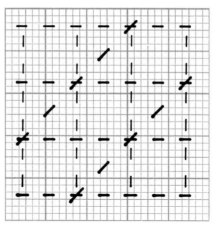

11. Sashiko squares crossed once, *3* and *9*. Note: This is the same as previously worked Sashiko squares crossed once except the crossing is in the opposite direction.

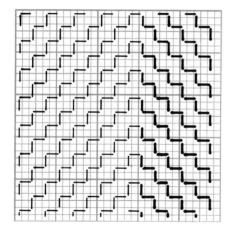

12. Sashiko steps, *4*, *6*, and *7*

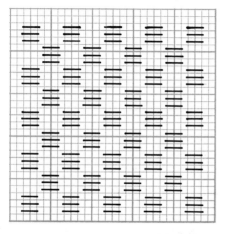

13. Kogin checks, *6*
Second Bargello Corner

Finishing and Trimming

Add trim to the fabric side of the vest before joining the sections. Sew tiny buttons at the intersections of the running stitches in Sashiko Pattern 5. Tack lace, then braid, over the dividing lines between the patterns. Join the seams and cover with braid. Bind the outer edges with foldover braid.

There are foldover braids available commercially, but it seems to me that something more special is required for all the time and care spent in embroidering the vest. I knitted a special braid for my vest and here are the simple knitting instructions for duplicating it.

I used several balls of Parisian cotton thread. You could also use DMC pearl cotton, size 3, in large balls. Use size 1 knitting needles. Cast on 10 stitches. Knit one row, purl one row. On all knit rows, knit two stitches together at the beginning, and increase one stitch on the next to last stitch. This will give you a bias strip. Knit strips to fit each area that is to be bound, or knit one continuous strip and machine stitch a row on each side of wherever you plan to cut.

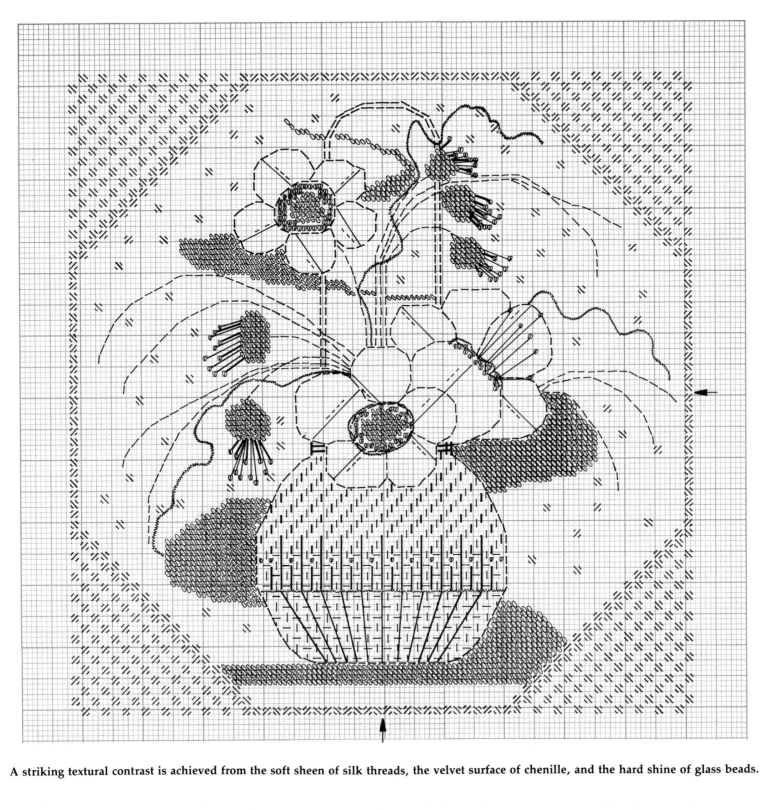

A striking textural contrast is achieved from the soft sheen of silk threads, the velvet surface of chenille, and the hard shine of glass beads.

Graph for Silken Flower Picture I

Key to Stitches, Picture I

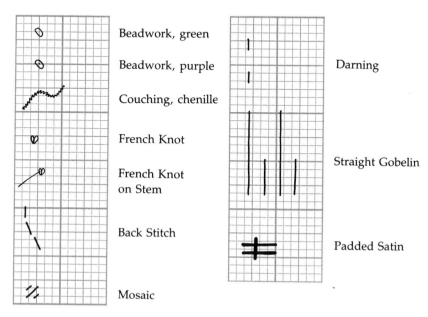

Beadwork, green

Beadwork, purple

Couching, chenille

French Knot

French Knot on Stem

Back Stitch

Mosaic

Darning

Straight Gobelin

Padded Satin

In addition to these graphs with their accompanying Keys to Stitches for Pictures I and II, you will find complete step-by-step instructions on the following pages. Study the color photographs in the color section of this book for further understanding of colors and stitches.

Materials Used in Both Flower Pictures

The tan canvas is Zweigart deluxe quality 13-mesh. It is cut 22 inches square and mounted on a stretcher bar frame of the same dimensions. Needles are sizes 20 and 22 tapestry; yarn darner, size 18, for Bullion Knots; sharp needle, size 8, beeswax, and ecru sewing silk thread for the beadwork.

Below is a list of the threads and beads. All of the silk threads are Soie d'Alger. They are used in the full seven ply, first separated and then laid flat, unless otherwise noted. DMC embroidery floss may be substituted, and it too should be handled in the same way.

Work the centers of the pictures first to keep the border stitching fresh.

Threads

1 Dull gold, 2243
2 Bright gold, 622
3 Rust, 2624
4 Light blue, 121
5 Lavender, 4631

6 Peach, 933
7 Ecru
8 Beige silk ribbon, ¹⁄₁₆ inch wide, Kanagawa 131

9 Rust silk chenille
10 Light blue silk chenille

Beads

11 Purple
12 White

13 Light blue
14 Medium green

Stitching Flower Picture I

Instructions on how to work stitches are found in the Dictionary of Stitches. Consult the Stitch Index on page 188. The **boldface italic** numbers placed after each step refer to the threads and beads in Materials Used for Both Flower Pictures.

Flowers

1. Work three flowers in *Padded Satin Stitch,* **4** and **5**.
2. Enter *Canvas Beadwork* in flower centers, **11**.
3. Work *French Knot* around the beading on the blue flowers, **5**. Fill the empty space completely. Space on graph left open for clarity.

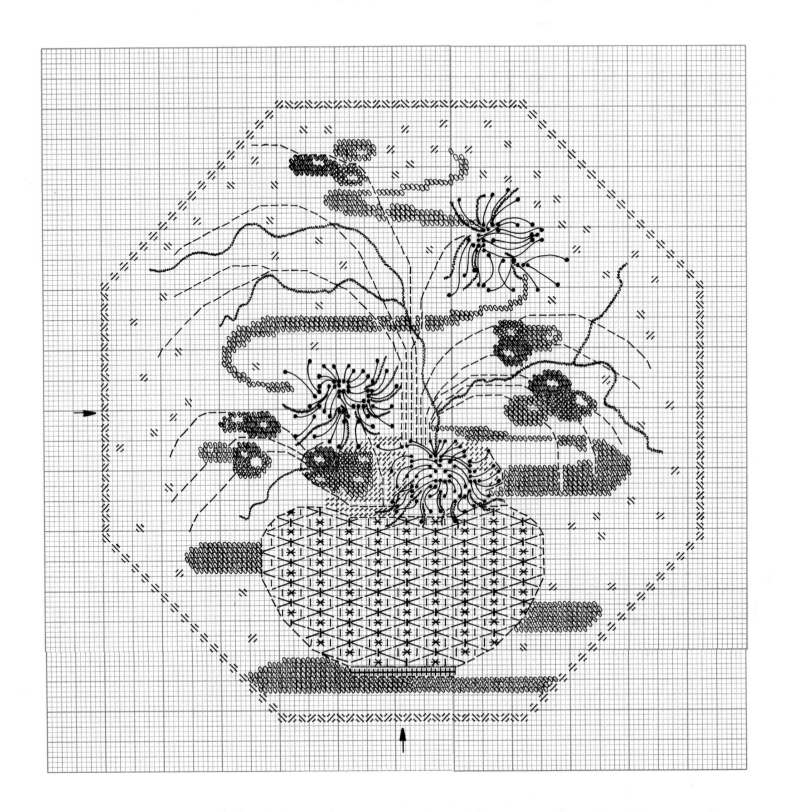

Graph for Silken Flower Picture II

Key to Stitches, Picture II

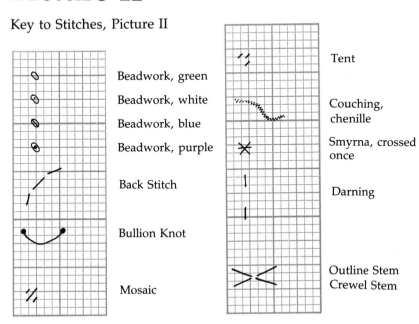

Beadwork, green	Tent
Beadwork, white	Couching, chenille
Beadwork, blue	
Beadwork, purple	Smyrna, crossed once
Back Stitch	Darning
Bullion Knot	
Mosaic	Outline Stem Crewel Stem

4. Work *French Knot* and *French Knot on Stem* on lavender flower, **4**.

5. Work *Couching* around *French Knot* on all three flowers, **9**, *Couching* down with 1-ply **3**.

6. Enter *Canvas Beadwork* for small flowers, **11**.

7. Work *Back Stitch* on stalks and stems, then *Outline Stem Stitch* over them, tightly twisted **1**.

8. Work *Whipped Stem Stitch* on flower stems, **2**.

9. Add *French Knot on Stem* to beaded flowers, **2** and **4**.

Basket

1. Enter *Back Stitch* outline of basket and handle, then *Crewel Stem Stitch* over it, tightly twisted **3**.

2. Work long *Straight Gobelin Stitch*, *French Knot*, and *Darning*, tightly twisted **3**.

3. Work remainder with *Darning*, **8**.

Background

1. Stitch *Canvas Beadwork* in the swirl design, **14**.

2. Work a solid border of *Mosaic Stitch* around the four sides. Leave matching open canvas spaces between the *Mosaic Stitch* in the four corner areas.

3. Work background in *Diagonal Tent Stitch*, scattering *Mosaic Stitch*, some slanting in one direction, some the other, **7**.

4. Work *Couching* on chenille twigs, **10**, couch down with 1-ply **4**.

Stitching Flower Picture II

Flowers

1. Work *Bullion Knot* flowers, **1, 2, 9, 4**, and **10**.

2. Work *French Knot* centers, **3** and **2**.

3. Enter *Canvas Beadwork* for small flowers, **12, 13**, and **14**.

4. Work *French Knot* in centers of small beaded flowers, **6**. (They are *not* shown on graph.)

5. Work *Back Stitch* on stalks and stems, *Outline Stem Stitch* over them, tightly twisted **1**.

6. Work *Whipped Stem Stitch* on flower stems, **2**.

Basket

1. Work *Back Stitch* outline of basket, then *Crewel Stem Stitch* over it, tightly twisted **3**.

2. Work diagonal lines, one direction *Outline Stem Stitch*, the other *Crewel Stem Stitch*, tightly twisted **3**.

3. Work *Darning* over the intersections of the diagonals in vertical rows, **8** (ribbon).

4. Work a *Smyrna*, crossed once, between the ribbon stitches, **3**.

5. Work a vertical row of *Darning* on either side of ribbon, **3**.

6. Work *Padded Satin Stitch* at the base of the basket.

7. Work *Couching* at the base, **9** couched down with 1-ply **3**.

Background

Same as for Picture I, except the chenille twigs are **9**, with 1-ply **3**.

Border Design for Both Silken Flower Pictures

This wide border consists of five different border treatments. See these tiers of borders and the placement of opposite corners in the color section.

The five borders of both pictures are the same except for the color changes stated below. The arrows indicate the center of the designs. Turn the work to complete all four corners. Note the graph for a second *Bargello* corner. This is shown because only opposite corners can match. See the photographs. Start the first of these five borders just outside the final line of Mosaic Stitch.

1. *False Gobelin* Border: Picture I, **9**; Picture II, **10**
2. *Buckey's Weaving* Border: Picture I, *Cross Stitch,* **1**; Picture II, *Cross Stitch,* **2**; Pictures I and II, *Darning,* tightly twisted **2**
*3. *Underside Couching* Chenille Border: Picture I, **9** couched down with 1-ply **3**; Picture II, **10** couched down with 1-ply **4**
4. *Slanting Gobelin* and *Mosaic* Border: Picture I, **3** and **4**; Picture II, **4** and **3**
5. *Bargello* Border: **1** and **2** with *Tent Stitch* background, **7**

*Work this step after you have worked steps 2 and 4.

Second Bargello Corner

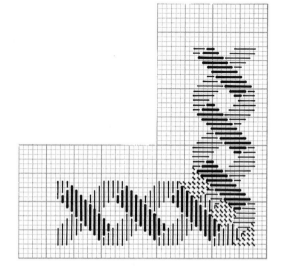

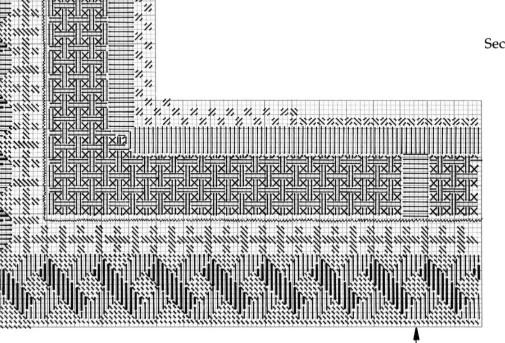

180

Alphabet Samplers

The letters pictured here are worked on 12-mesh canvas with outlines and shadows stitched in dark shades of 2-ply Persian or 4-ply Nantucket Twist. They are highlighted with touches of French silk. These letters may also be worked on finer canvas with delicate colors, or rug canvas with bolder colors.

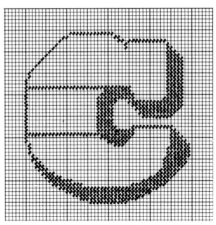

1. Rococo Stitch.
2. Eyelet Stitch in center, outlined with Slanting Gobelin and Back Stitch, each worked in two directions, on Tent Stitch ground, also worked in two directions. Eyelet is overstitched on completion.
3. Hungarian Ground.

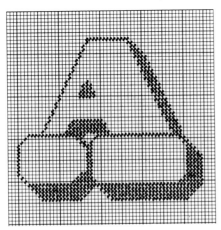

1. Parisian Stitch.
2. Scottish Stitch; Flat Stitch portion worked in alternate directions.
3. Shell Stitch.

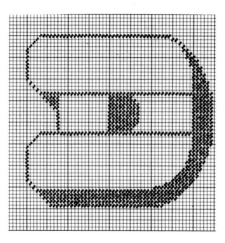

1. Hungarian Diamond backstitched in diagonal rows.
2. Tied Oblong Cross Stitch in center outlined with Back Stitch; Cross Stitch at top and bottom.
3. Tent Stitch.
4. Cushion Stitch outlined with Back Stitch, alternating with boxes of Tent.

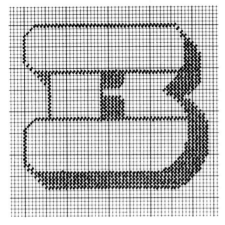

1. Leaf Stitch on Tent Stitch ground.
2. Diamond Eyelet Stitch on Tent Stitch ground.
3. Mosaic Stitch worked in boxes.
4. Byzantine Stitch.

1. Moorish Stitch.
2. Flat Stitch in corner (direction of stitch reversed). Straight Gobelin Stitch worked in two directions.
3. Flat Stitch (direction of stitch reversed).
4. Encroaching Gobelin Stitch with blending.

181

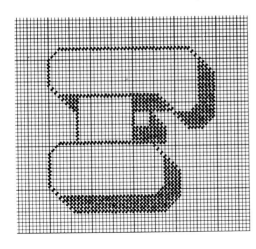

1. Wave Stitch.
2. St. George and St. Andrew Cross Stitch; single row of vertical Tent Stitch.
3. Leviathan Stitch.
4. Slanting Gobelin Stitch outlining Flat Stitch panes.

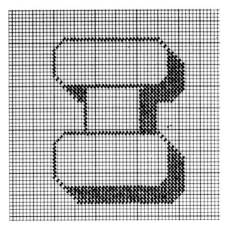

1. Reversed Tent Stitch striping; Straight Gobelin Stitch worked in two directions for border; Tent Stitch corners; Back Stitch outline.
2. Triple Cross Stitch in center on Tent Stitch ground, outlined with Reversed Tent Stitch and Back Stitch; Smyrna Stitch corners.
3. Shaded Flat Stitch outlined with vertical and horizontal Slanting Gobelin Stitch.

1. Kalem Stitch in vertical rows with blending.
2. Eyelet Stitch alternating with boxes of Mosaic Stitch; row of horizontal Tent Stitch at top.
3. Kalem Stitch in horizontal rows.
4. Vertical and horizontal Cashmere Stitch with Smyrna Stitch at intersections; panes of Tent Stitch.

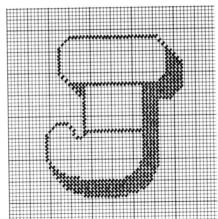

1. Alternate squares of Tent Stitch outlined with Slanting Gobelin and Flat Stitch outlined with Tent Stitch. The Flat Stitch square is made and then the unit is reworked in opposite direction.
2. Shaded Knotted Stitch.
3. Long-armed Cross Stitch.

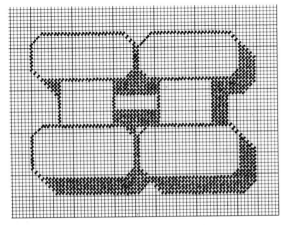

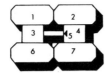

1. Small Chequer Stitch partially outlined with Tent Stitch.
2. Small Chequer Stitch partially outlined with Tent Stitch.
3. Wave Stitch parted in middle by vertical Chain Stitch.
4. Wave Stitch parted in middle by vertical Chain Stitch.
5. Horizontal Chain Stitch.
6. Slanting Gobelin Stitch in center with Small Chequer Stitch at sides; Tent Stitch ground.
7. Large Chequer Stitch with Tent Stitch outline.

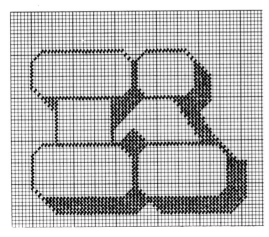

1. Turkey Knot on Tent Stitch ground.
2. From center out: Tent Stitch, Hungarian Stitch, and Mosaic Stitch on Tent Stitch ground.
3. Greek Stitch.
4. Alternate rows of Plait and Tent Stitch.
5. Oblong Cross Stitch alternating with Smyrna Stitch (not crossed horizontally).
6. Continuous Flat Stitch outlined with Mosaic Stitch on Tent Stitch ground.

1. Surrey Stitch fringe with row of Long-armed Cross Stitch at top and Tent Stitch at bottom.
2. Web Stitch.
3. Bargello.

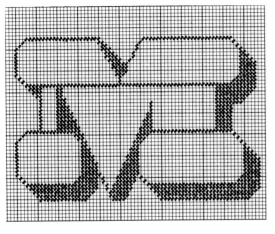

1. Large and Upright Cross Stitch, four Back Stitches at intersections.
2. Shaded Gobelin Plait Stitch.
3. Slanting Gobelin Stitch in vertical rows.
4. Bargello, 4.2 step; alternate rows 2.2 step.
5. Fishbone Stitch.
6. Continuous Cashmere Stitch (direction reversed).
7. Continuous Cashmere Stitch.

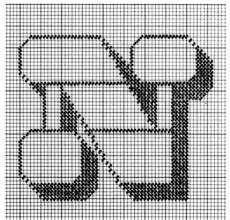

1. Oblong Cross Stitch tied down with Back Stitch; Upright Cross Stitch in between.
2. Alternate boxes of Leviathan and Mosaic Stitch overstitched with Upright Cross; Back Stitch around boxes, Tent and Reversed Tent Stitch at sides.
3. Plait Stitch.
4. Continuous Mosaic Stitch.
5. Plait Stitch.
6. Stem Stitch with Tent Stitch at top and sides.
7. Cross Stitch with Smyrna Stitch at regular intervals.

Omit tail of Q to make O.

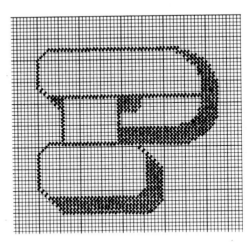

1. Narrow stripes: horizontal Straight Gobelin and Smyrna Stitches. Wider stripes: vertical Straight Gobelin.
2. Large two-color Leviathan Stitch with Cross Stitch at center; outlined with Tent Stitch.
3. Parisian Stitch.
4. Hungarian Stitch.

183

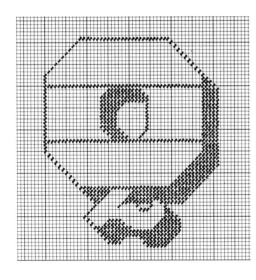

1. Shaded horizontal Brick Stitch.
2. Straight Gobelin Stitch between rows of Oblong Cross Stitch; Back Stitch between rows.
3. Same as 2.
4. Blended vertical Brick Stitch.
5. Tent Stitch.

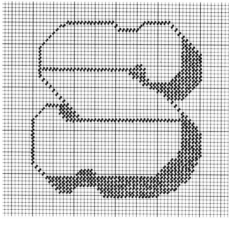

1. Alternate boxes of Tent and Mosaic Stitch.
2. Jacquard Stitch.
3. Rounded Wave Stitch.

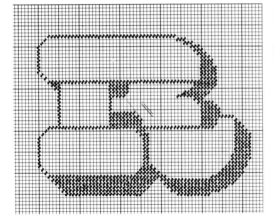

1. Hungarian Stitch.
2. Algerian Eye Stitch in corners with Eyelet Stitch in center, Tent Stitch boxes.
3. Parisian Stitch.
4. Horizontal and vertical Straight Gobelin Stitch, worked over Tramé; Back Stitch between outer rows.
5. Tent Stitch with Slanting Gobelin Stitches used at random to create rain effect.

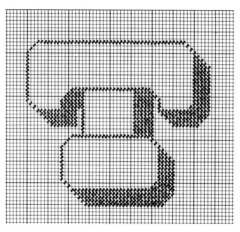

1. Leaf Stitch on Tent Stitch ground.
2. Central motif of Slanting Gobelin in two directions. Cross Stitch in center; Tent Stitch ground, Back Stitch on either side.
3. Continuous Mosaic Stitch.

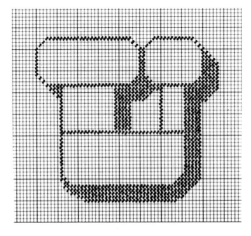

1. Shaded Encroaching Gobelin Stitch with Back Stitch at top and bottom.
2. Double Cross Stitch.
3. Leviathan Stitch overstitched with Triple Cross Stitch; Tent Stitch panes.
4. French Stitch outlined with Back Stitch.
5. Byzantine Stitch.

184

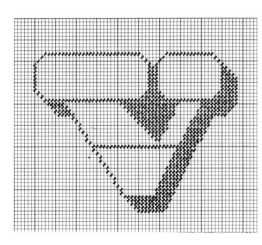

1. Triangle Stitch with Smyrna Stitch at corners; Back Stitch outlines.
2. Leviathan Stitch in center; Smyrna Stitch; Tent Stitch ground; Back Stitch outlines.
3. Continuous Mosaic Stitch.
4. Double and Tie Stitch.
5. Reversed Tent Stitch.

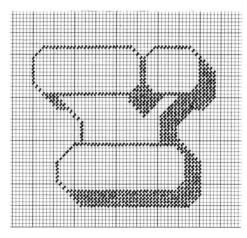

1. Bargello.
2. Moorish Stitch.
3. Long-armed Cross Stitch.
4. Crossed Corners Stitch with Back Stitch between rows.

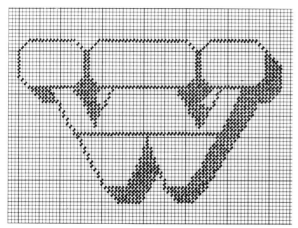

1. Cushion Stitch.
2. Oriental Stitch.
3. Large Chequer Stitch; Flat Stitch portion overstitched in silk.
4. Slanting Gobelin Stitch, Back Stitch between rows.
5. Blended horizontal Tent Stitch.
6. Blended horizontal Tent Stitch.

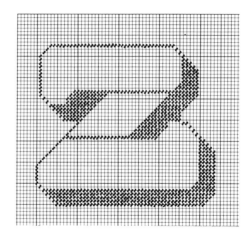

1. Milanese Stitch.
2. Hungarian Stitch.
3. Bargello.

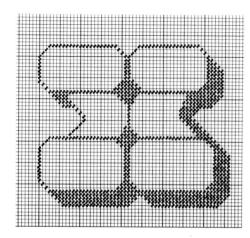

1. Hungarian Stitches form diamonds, Slanting Gobelin x's; Bargello worked in one color and overstitched in contrasting color at top and bottom.
2. Stem Stitch.
3. Upright Cross Stitch.
4. Horizontal rows of Back Stitch.
5. Reversed Tent Stitch, Back-stitched at intersections.
6. Horizontal Cashmere Stitch.

BIBLIOGRAPHY

Ambuter, Carolyn. *The Open Canvas*. New York: Workman Publishing, 1982.

Cox, Hebe. *Canvas Embroidery*. London: Mills and Boone, Ltd., 1960.

deDillmont, Thérèse. *Encyclopedia of Needlework*. Mulhouse, France: Editions Th. de Dillmont, 1880.

Enthoven, Jacqueline. *Stitches with Variations*. Livermore, California: Aardvark, 1985.

———. *The Stitches of Creative Embroidery*. New York: Van Nostrand Rheinhold, 1964.

Gibbon, M.A. *Canvas Work*. London: G.G. Bell and Sons, Ltd., 1965.

Hanley, Hope. *Needlepoint*. New York: Charles Scribner's Sons, 1964.

Ireys, Katherine. *Canvas Embroidery Stitch Patterns*. New York: Thomas Y. Crowell Company, 1964.

John, Edith. *Creative Stitches*. New York: Dover Publications, Inc., 1973.

King, Bucky. *Creative Canvas Embroidery*. New York: Hearthside Press, Inc., 1963.

Markrich, Lilo. *Principles of the Stitch*. Chicago: Henry Regnery Company, 1976.

Rhodes, Mary. *Ideas for Canvas Work*. Newton, Massachusetts: Charles T. Batsford, Ltd., 1970.

Snook, Barbara. *Florentine Embroidery*. New York: Charles T. Scribner's Sons, 1967.

Thomas. Mary. *Dictionary of Embroidery Stitches*. London: Hodder and Stoughton, Ltd., 1965.

SUPPLIERS

Aardvark, P.O. Box 2449, Livermore, CA 94550. (retail)
  Natesh rayon thread
  Belding Corticelli silk sewing thread
  Novelty beads
American Crewel and Canvas, P.O. Box 453, Canastota, NY 13032. (wholesale and retail)
  Zweigart canvas
  Paternayan Persian
  Nantucket Twist
  Medicis crewel wool
  DMC threads
  Gold tinsel thread
  Gold Lumiyarn braid
  Mill Hill Graphics seed beads
  Stretcher bars
  Linen thread
Aurora Silk, Cheryl Kolander Williams, 5806 N. Vancouver Avenue, Portland, OR 97217. (wholesale and retail)
  Hand-dyed silk thread
  Silk chenille
Fleur De Paris, 10331 W. Jefferson Boulevard, Culver City, CA 90230. (wholesale)
  Zweigart canvas
  DMC threads
  Medicis crewel wool
Hansi's Haus, 35 Fairfield Place, West Caldwell, NJ 07006. (retail)
  Zweigart canvas
  Dirty linen (rustic canvas)
  Linen thread
  Mill Hill Graphics seed beads
Kreinik Mfg. Co. Inc., P.O. Box 1966, Parkersburg, WV 26102. (wholesale)
  Au Ver A Soie French silk
  Silk chenille, special orders
  Metal threads of all kinds, including blending filament, passing
      thread, braids, and cords

  Silk gauze and Siltek canvas
  Au Ver A Soie Hand Creme
M. and J. Trimming Co., 1008 Sixth Avenue, New York, NY 10018. (wholesale and retail)
  Soutache braid, braids and trims of all descriptions
Needle-Ease, 81 Uplands Drive, West Hartford, CT 06107. (wholesale and retail)
  Enlarger-Lite
Quadrum, Route 1, Thomaston, ME 04855
  Cairo matte cotton
Straw into Gold, 3006 San Pablo Avenue, Berkeley, CA 94702. (wholesale)
  Soie Crystale Italian silk floss
Talas, 213 West 35 Street, New York, NY 10001
  Orvis soap
Joan Toggitt, Ltd., 35 Fairfield Place, West Caldwell, NJ 07006. (wholesale)
  Zweigart canvas
  Dirty linen (rustic canvas)
  Linen thread
  Mill Hill Graphics seed beads
Wichelt Imports, Inc., Hwy. 35, Stoddard, WI 54658. (wholesale)
  Congress Cloth, 16-mesh (used for vest)
YLI Corp., 45 West 300 North, Provo, UT 84601. (wholesale and retail)
  Kanagawa silk embroidery thread
  Kanagawa silk ribbon

INDEX OF STITCH NAMES

Numbers in *italic* refer to illustrations.

INDEX

Numbers in *italic* refer to illustrations.